Dave Etter

SUNFLOWER COUNTY

SPOON RIVER POETRY PRESS
1994

Back cover photo by Patricia Clewell.

Published by Spoon River Poetry Press, David Pichaske, editor; P.O. Box 6, Granite Falls, Minnesota 56258.

ISBN 0-944024-24-6

1   2   3   4   93   94   95   96   97   98

Dave Etter

SUNFLOWER COUNTY

Acknowledgments

Most of these poems have appeared in *Alliance, Illinois* (Kylix Press, 1978), *Cornfields* (Spoon River Poetry Press, 1980), *West of Chicago* (Spoon River Poetry Press, 1981), *Alliance, Illinois* (Spoon River Poetry Press, 1983), *Midlanders* (Spoon River Poetry Press, 1988), and *Electric Avenue* (Spoon River Poetry Press, 1988). Several poems have appeared in *Crabtree's Woman* (BkMk Press, 1972), *Bright Mississippi* (Juniper Press, 1975), *Central Standard Time* (BkMk Press, 1978), *Open to the Wind* (Uzzano Press, 1978), *Riding the Rock Island Through Kansas* (Wolfsong, 1979), and *Voyages to the Inland Sea* (University of Wisconsin—La Crosse).

Poems in this book have also appeared in the following publications: *Abraxas, Ann Arbor Review, Applecart, Ark River Review, Back Door, Beacon News* (Aurora, Illinois), *Carbuncle, The Chariton Review, Chicago Review, Chicago Tribune Magazine, Chouteau Review, The Chowder Review, Cincinnati Poetry Review, Coal City Review, Colorado State Review, Cottonwood Review, Cream City Review, Cutbank, Dacotah Territory, December, The Dragonfly, The Elburn Herald, Eleven, Elkhorn Review, English Journal, Epos, The Far Point* (Canada), *Focus/Midwest, Foxway, Giants Play Well in the Drizzle, The Great Lakes Review, The Greenfield Review, The Harrison Street Review, Hearse, Hiram Poetry Review, Icarus, Illinois Quarterly, Images, Indiana Review, The Kansas City Star, Kansas Quarterly, The Lake Superior Review, The Laurel Review, Long Pond Review, The Madison Review, Mid-American Review, Midwest, Midwest Poetry Review, The Midwest Quarterly, The Minnesota Review, Mississippi Valley Review, The Nation, Nebraska Review, The Nebraska Review* (University of Nebraska—Omaha), *Nebraska Territory, New: American and Canadian Poetry, New Letters, The New Moon, New Tomorrow, New Work/s* (Duck Down Press), *The North American Review, North Dakota Quarterly, Northeast, Northern Lights, The North Stone Review, Oakwood, The Ohio Review, Open Places, The Panhandler, Panorama (Chicago Daily News), Paragon* (Kaneland High School Literary Annual), *Pebble, Peninsula Review, Poet & Critic, Poetry, Poetry Northwest, Poetry Now, Practices of the Wind, Prairie Schooner, Quartet, Raccoon, Rain, Rapport, River Bottom, The Salt Creek Reader, Salt Lick, Shenandoah, Siftings from the Clearing, Slow Dancer* (England), *South Dakota Review, South Florida Poetry Journal, Sou'wester, The Spoon River Quarterly, Stinktree, Stuffed Crocodile, Sumac, Sun, Tennessee Poetry Journal, Three Rivers Poetry Journal, Today, TriQuarterly, Uzzano, Wells Elevator, Wind, Wisconsin Review, The Writers' Bar-B-Q, Writers' Forum, Yarrow,* and *Zone 3*.

To Peggy, Emily, George, and Michael

CONTENTS

GEORGE MAXWELL: County Seat 1

CHESTER GREENE: Taking the Census 3

HENRY LICHENWALNER: Living in the Middle 4

ANDY HASSELGARD: Gone with the Grain 5

DOC MITCHELL: Windy 6

ERNIE KEEPNEWS: Then and Now 7

WENDY OLSON: Drought 8

MITCH VALENTINE: Billboard 10

WADE HOLLENBACH: Hard Cider 11

APRIL McINTYRE: Fishing in the Rain 12

RED RADER: Electric Avenue 13

BRIAN HARDY: Little Theater 14

OLIVER BRIGGS: Night Work 16

CHRISTOPHER MOORE: Lionel the Cat 17

LIZ ALTENBERGER: Rose Tattoo 18

BRUCE PUTNAM: Crayola 20

ELWOOD COLLINS: Summer of 1932 21

LESTER RASMUSSEN: Jane's Blue Jeans 22

VALERIE MAYHEW: Cornfield Virgin 23

SHEENA FITZGERALD: Pisces Sun 24

TANYA OWENS: Wrestler 25

HATTIE EAKINS: V-J Day 26

REX AGEE: Getting at the Truth 28

LEE GUTHRIE: Country Smoke 29

TUCKER STONE: Stuttering Hands 30

ORVILLE JUMP: Me, Myself, and I 31

MARY ANN CLEMENS: Sheet Music 32

ANGELA KNIGHT: Hot Rod 33

SUSAN COBB: Names 34

NICHOLAS HOBSON: Juney Love 35

ROGER POWELL: The Talk at Rukenbrod's 36

FLORA RUTHERFORD: Postcard to Florida 38

HARRY KRENCHICKI: Tallgrass Township 39

DAWN CASAGRANDE: Concert   40

LUKE HENNESSEY: Time Clock   41

STANLEY ADAMS: County Road K   42

WILLIAM GOODENOW: The Red Depot   43

JAMIE McFEE: Big Sister   44

SAL BIVIANO: Pennies   46

MELISSA JENKINS: Staring into Winter   47

YVONNE WYNCOOP: Looking at Clouds   48

FRANK TEMPLE: Wet Spring, Dark Earth   49

DANIEL KORNBLUM: Bad News   50

ROY ORSULAK: An Ordinary Sinner   51

MOLLY DUNAWAY: Rainbow   52

ZACHARY GRANT: Guilt   53

NEIL CAMPBELL: Humor   54

STUBBY PAYNE: Stocking Tops   55

AMBER WHEATLEY: Out to Lunch   56

FORREST DAY: Reds   57

MADELINE KUCHARIK: Devotion   58

JESSIE LONDON: Keeping On   60

VERONICA BROOKS: Jogging   61

SISSY RICHARDSON: Bubble Gum   62

NINA JAMES: Writing Down the Dream   63

GABE INGELS: Jazz Night   64

DARLENE WINTERS: Funeral Home   65

HORACE LOVEJOY: Abraham Lincoln   66

MELVIN TIKOO: Rocking   68

LONNIE EVANS: Diminuendo in Green   69

PATRICK HANIFAN: Scarecrow   70

WAT NUGENT: Epitaph   71

SHERMAN CARTER: Bikinis   72

AMOS BLACKBURN: War of the Hybrids   74

DIANE GUBICZA: Spanish Peanuts   75

ELEANOR ASHBY: Thinking of Cancer   76

MATT ROLLINS: A Chicago Romance   77

CAROL PARMALEE: Foreclosure   78

JUSTIN UHLENHAKE: Tickets 80

CLARENCE FOWLER: Nuts and Bolts 81

TRACY LIMANTOUR: Flowers and Smoke 82

VANCE DOUGLAS: Rain Check 83

CRAIG BARNET: Tune Box 84

JOSHUA KING: Bread and Apples 85

DREW MANNING: Harvest Dust 86

ABIGAIL TAYLOR: Senility 87

HAZEL JORDAN: Puberty 88

PRUDENCE ARCHER: Thirteen 90

ISAIAH ROODHOUSE:
Putting Off the Encyclopedia Salesman 91

KYLE TROWBRIDGE: Bird's-Eye View 92

PIKE WALDROP: For the Record 93

MICHAEL FLANAGAN: Unemployed 94

WHITEY PHILLIPS: The Red Dress 96

GARY SHACKHAMMER: Remembering the Thirties 97

CHICK CUNNINGHAM: Horse Opera 98

STELLA LYNCH: The Opposite Sex 99

DAVID MOSS: Corn and Beans 100

ROXANNE RUSSELL: Getting Caught 101

EDGAR WILSON: Carousel 102

MICHELLE TREMBLAY: Yellow 104

REV. FELIX DIETRICH: Gospel 105

VICKI ST. CLAIR: Home from the River 106

TRAVIS JOHNSTON: North 107

RANDY WHITE: From a Big Chief Tablet
Found Under a Bench at the Courthouse Square 108

BREW AMES: Boogers 109

SHERRY LARKIN: Two on the Farm 110

BRIDGET RICE: Motorcycle Accident 111

LILLIAN EDWARDS: In Fear of Old Age 112

HOWARD DRUMGOOLE: Hotel Tall Corn 113

CLIFF PECOTA: Mud, Oil, and Jello 114

JEREMY FORQUER: The Smell of Lilacs 116

ARDIS NEWKIRK: At the Charity Ball 117

GARTH LIGHT: Muscles   118

RICHARD GARLAND: Railroad Strike   119

CHARLOTTE NORTHCOTT: Insomnia   120

JUNIOR IVES: Barn Burner   121

LOGAN STUART: The Union Soldier   122

BARBARA HAWKINS: Anteaters   124

PEGGY DANIELS: Moonlight Yodel   125

SHIRLEY JELLICOE: Neighbor   126

MAURY CHASE: Famous   127

SONNY BAXTER: Spider Webs   128

KENNETH SANDSTROM: Crazy in California   130

DUKE NICHOLS: Domestic   131

TOM RANDALL: Under a Gigantic Sky   132

VERNON YATES: Talking About the Erstwhile
    Paperboy to the Editor of the *Alliance Gazette*   133

URSULA ZOLLINGER: Last House on Union Street   134

GLENN TWITCHELL: Rose Petals   135

PERRY MEEK: Wife Killer   136

DENISE WATKINS: Some Come Running   137

JUBAL MONTGOMERY: Oddball   138

WALLY DODGE: The Hat   139

MONICA ROBERTS: Private Dancer   140

AUGUST CRABTREE: Simple Words   142

DR. MALCOLM LINDSAY: Catfish and Watermelon   143

RUDY GERSTENBERG: Memo to the Erie Lackawanna   144

MARSHALL COOPER: Weeping   145

LUCY BETH YOUNGQUIST: Thanksgiving   146

EMMETT BEASLEY: Man Talking to Himself   147

JOHNNY WILCOX: In the Barbershop   148

ANGEL LOOK: Chicken Milk   149

TRUDY MONROE: Saturday Afternoon on Elm Street   150

GROVER ELY: Ancestral Home   151

DEXTER CADY: Calves   152

SARAH MULLEN: Visiting Writer   153

JOE SPRAGUE: Fourteen Stones   154

HERBERT TOMPKINS: The Crippled Poet's Dream   155

CLEO BOONE: Golden Wedding Anniversary   156

NOAH CREEKMORE: Bingo   157

POP GAINES: After the Farm Auction   158

YALE BROCKLANDER: Tractor on Main Street   159

BLAKE SAMUELS: Chain Saw   160

RONALD OSTERLE: Blackboard   162

TIMOTHY PARKER: Crossing Gates   163

FLOYD NYE: Dog on the Stairs   164

DEWEY CLAY DOYLE: Sleeping Bags   165

LOUISE CATHCART: Hearing an Old Song Again   166

MARCUS MILLSAP: School Day Afternoon   167

HAROLD BLISS: Questions and Answers   168

SAMANTHA TATE: Wet Towels   169

ERIC PECKENPAUGH: Toy Soldiers   170

PEARL INGERSOLL: Homework   171

LUCKY SCHU: A Fool in Love   172

NELSON HURLBUT: Last Day of Summer Vacation, 1934   174

STEPHEN FROMHOLD: Freight Trains in Winter   175

CURLY VANCE: The Pool Players   176

MISSY UMBARGER: Stories in the Kitchen   178

EUGENE CLARK: Grass Roots   179

ZOLA THOMAS: The Woman in the Rented Room   180

DALE SUNDBERG: Fir Tree   181

LYNNE MOSEBY: Piano   182

ALAN COMSTOCK: Old Man   183

JUDY WYCKOFF: Howling Walter   184

MARTY HUBBARD: Four Bottles of White Wine   185

BOOTH SCHOFIELD: A Dream of Old   186

CANDY MIZEROCK: Blues Alphabet   188

NETTIE KERSHAW: Pickle Puss   189

OSCAR CHEATHAM: Scotch Pine   190

ROMA HIGGINS: Cricket   191

AVERY LUCAS: Apples   192

DELBERT VARNEY: One-Way Conversation
with a Rug Beater   193

KARL THEIS: The Widower Turns Eighty   194

SHELLEY BROWN: Acorns   195

CHARLEY HOOPER: Schoolteacher   196

MILO FERRIS: A Damned Pretty Rain   197

LYLE MURPHY: Pregnant   198

TERRY REESE: Boom Boom on B Street   199

CASEY DIXON: Moony   200

ALICIA JACKSON: Fire Dream   202

IRWIN STREETER: Worms   203

HARLAN ADCOCK: Body   204

GERTRUDE VON ERICH: School Board   205

FRED DELOPLAINE: Illinois Farmers   206

EDWINA McBRIDE: Trademarks   207

AARON FICKLIN: Brother   208

MAX VERDERBER: Ausagaunaskee   210

DAISY PETTIGREW: Carnival on Eye Street   211

JEROME HOLTSAPPLE: Flower Thief   212

KEVIN PRUITT: Taking Down the Flag   213

CLYDE ROCKWELL: Bus Stop   214

RACHEL OSGOOD: Cornhusk Dolls   215

PATRICIA WELLS: Picking the Garbage   216

NED SWIFT: Downtown   217

ANTHONY FASANO: Greenhorn   218

CRYSTAL GAVIS: Depressed After Being Fired
    from Another Job   220

URBIE TUCKER: Wild Asparagus   221

L. D. McDOWELL: Apprentice Plumber   222

BECKY FARMER: Seen and Not Heard   223

HERSCHEL NIEDERCORN: Requiem   224

TERESA BIRDSELL: Sunflower Queen   225

SCOOTER HARGROVE: Punch Bowl   226

JEFFREY KOHRS: Summer Employment   227

BOOG MONCRIEF: Falling Apart   228

PAUL SUMMERHAY: Manuscript   229

GRETCHEN NAYLOR: Cloakrooms   230

DENNY GRIMES: Winged Seeds   231

KERRY WOODRUFF: Nicolette   232

JUDGE EMIL ZANGWILL: Angry Words   233

CARL YELENICH: One Tough Hombre   234

BEN HILDEBRAND: Father and Son   235

DANIELLE BLUE: Child Abuse   236

MASON SINCENDIVER: Driving to Town   238

WOODY O'NEILL: Outside the Western Auto Store   239

MILES POTTER: Spooks   240

DEREK VREELAND: The Apple Trees of Pioneer Grove   241

SANDRA SIGAFOOSE: Newcomer   242

TODD LANPHERE: Ice Cream Store   243

KIM AUSTIN: Art Class   244

LARRY GRAHAM: Empty Beer Can   245

JIMMY WINGATE: Cob Shed   246

AMANDA PURTILL: Four Rows of Sweet Corn   248

RILEY NOVAK: Tables and Chairs   249

CAMILLE WEBSTER: Bull Durham   250

THAD STEPHENS: "In the Mood"   251

EMILY DETWEILER: Lyman's Way   252

VINCENT PEREZ: Sailor   254

DUANE FORBES: Buffalo Nickel   255

RALPH C. KRAMER: Gossip   256

SCOTT LANSING: Trotters   258

ADAM POSEY: Sunday Comics   259

OTIS K. SIZEMORE: Child in the House   260

FAYE HOCKING: At the Home for Unwed Mothers   261

LANCE BOOMSMA: Wedding Reception   262

DAISY COLE: The Housekeeper's Story   263

BOYD DRAKE: Staying Up Late   264

JANICE NELSON: Community Hospital   265

BRANDON OLDFATHER: Spittoon   266

WARREN EGGLESTON: Nostalgia   267

KEITH APPLEBEE: Boozing Bigots   268

O. E. MOONEY: Working on the Railroad   269

NADINE ORLANDINI: Half a Loaf   270

IVAN LOOMIS: The Vision 271

FANCY SCARBOROUGH: Osage Orange 272

JOLENE DOERR: Fat 273

TY JARVIS: Talkers 274

PHYLLIS NESBIT: Chinese Restaurant 276

HOPE GIBBS: Fire and Water 277

ROBERT EVERWINE: Son 278

NATHAN ACKERMAN: In Kreb's Kandy Kitchen 279

GRACE RODZINSKY: Cocktail Party 280

CORKY NOLAN: High School Blues 281

PHIL DUDLEY: Cow in the Creek 282

LEWIS PERCY: Goodbye 283

WYNTON THATCHER: Duets 284

BILLY UNDERWOOD: Memorial Day 285

IRIS EXLEY: Things and Stuff 286

ROWENA STARK: Snowman 288

HERMAN FOX: Happy Hour 289

BARRY MACMILLAN: Cold Front 290

CLARK SPRINGSTEAD: Fender Sitting 291

LISA GENTRY: Last Morning 292

IRENE KOZAK: Telephone 294

SAM BUCKNER: Lovers' Quarrel 295

NORBERT JOYCE: Drummers 296

SEAN KANE: At the Eighth-Grade Dancing Class 298

MARJORIE YORK: Brown 299

ESTELLE ETHEREGE: Seventy-Five 300

WILBURN MILLER: Bud 301

HEIDI KOENIG: Slow Day at the Office 302

SELMA SKOGLAND: Peanut Butter 303

DOUG CHANDLER: Television 304

GUY HANSEN: Retirement 305

AMY GOGARTY: Dimples 306

LUANNE ELLIOTT: Escaping the Holy Rollers 307

TROY BOWMAN: Forgiven 308

EDWARD FINLEY: Don't Stop the Carnival 309

WENDELL MAGEE: Second Shift at the Printing Plant   310
GENEVIEVE SNYDER: Vacationland   311
ARCHIE HAMILTON: Tale of the Tub   312
FERN DYSART: Ninety-Two in the Shade   314
MACK SCARCE: Going Steady   315
RUTH ULRICH: Baby   316
VELMA WITHERSPOON: Mischief   317
BARNEY PRINGLE: Heat Wave   318
OWEN HENDERSON: Bad Night on Blue Hollow Road   319
KELSEY JUDD: Murder   320
CONNIE CARPENTER: Gold   321
RUBY KIMBLE: Homecoming Game   322
DONALD GUEST: Boredom   323
BEVERLY LOMAX: Shipping Clerk   324
LINDA FULGHAM: Ida May and Ida May Not   326
JENNIFER PARSONS: Lemonade   327
AUDREY SMITH: Opinion   328
RYAN HILL: Neighborhood   329
JULIE MARSHALL: In Therapy   330
BRADFORD TULLEY: Lonesome   331
MAYNARD LEWIS: Kafka   332
PETER VOSBURGH: Return to River Street   333
STEPHANIE MORAN: Sad   334
ELLIS BUTTERFIELD: Leaning Barn   335
HOLLY JO ANDERSON: Bein' Poor   336
TOOKIE THORNHILL: Cleaning Up the Yard   337
ELLEN OPDYCKE: Husband   338
GERALD WAGNER: Student   339
MURRAY HARRIS: Fall of 1956   340
EILEEN CHRISTENSEN: Class Reunion   342
LAMAR WOCKENFUSS: Friendly Persuasion   343
JASON FOSTER: Impotence   344
IRMA GILLESPIE: Chicken Bone   345
WESLEY HARKNESS: Why He Didn't Repair the Bookcase   346
VON BIGELOW: Screwdrivers   347

SIDNEY LANE: Friend to Friend   348

GORDON DALRYMPLE: Having Fun with Dick and Jane   350

LLOYD KELLOGG: The Man Who Played Clarinet in the
  High School Band Back in 1936, but Then Never
  Amounted to Anything Much After That,
  Is Here Again Today, Folks   351

ALEX WRIGHT: Opera House   352

CLAIRE LANCASTER: Ice and Snow   353

ISABEL OGDEN: Redneck   354

JACQUELINE NERVAL: Trash   355

BUDDY AZZOLINA: Suicide Note   356

FRANCES BELLAMY: White Man's Flies   357

RITA OBERKFELL: Eight O'clock in the Evening   358

SYLVESTER F. BILLINGS: The Civil War   359

HELEN ABERNATHY: Animal Shelter   360

GILBERT HUTCHINSON: Toilet Paper   362

ERIKA FONTANA: Parties   363

LUCILLE SCRIBNER: Diary   364

OZZIE NAVARRO: Just the Facts   366

BONNIE ARNELL: A Motherless Child   367

NOLA GARRISON: Composition   368

SALLY WHIPPLE: Great-Grandmother's Speech on
  New Year's Eve   370

MILDRED CESAREK: At the Crossroads   371

KATHY SCHOONOVER: Foreign Affairs   372

GREGORY DAWSON: Sick Before Supper   373

DEENA FERACA: Child Molester   374

JILL CORBETT: Rocking Horse   376

KIRK GEARHART: Diesels   377

RUSSELL HAYES: Federal Highway   378

LUTHER WILHELM: Nightmare   379

CYNTHIA RAINES: Silent   380

PORTER KNOX: The Christmas Tree   381

MILTON CAVANAUGH: Scratch   382

CHRISTINE ANDREWS: Company Lunchroom   383

KERMIT OLMSTED: Roots   384

CALVIN FAIRBANKS: Letter to Grandma   385

REGINA WASHINGTON: Incompatibility   386

LOLA FOWLES: Guitar Strings   387

JACY LAMONICA: Coy   388

ELMER PRATT: Revelation   389

ADELAIDE CRAWFORD: Initiation   390

CURTIS LURTSEMA: National Pastime   391

BUCKY ATWOOD: Coming Down   392

ROSCOE VAUGHAN: All Things to All People   393

ERIN KAISER: North Woods   394

SHELDON MERCER: Common Sense   395

GLORIA HAWTHORNE: Her Dying Child   396

ARNOLD WHEELER: Ambition   397

PHOEBE YAEGER: Cheerleader   398

LEONARD MASSINGAIL: Fatherly Advice   399

CLAUDE ROSE: Deluge   400

KATE PINCHOT: Public Library   402

RAYMOND HARPER: Clowns   404

MICKEY CONWAY: Tornado Warning   405

PAMELA DOOLEY: Subdivision   406

GOLDIE KLIPSTEIN: Creative Writing   407

BRENT PICCONY: Athlete   408

NANCY EASTWICK: Jericho Township   410

KAREN HICKS: Loony   411

GWEN PETERSON: Sun Belt   412

MAYBELLE JONES: A Trip to the Bank   413

JACK ERTEL: The Fighter   414

EARL VAN HORNE: Monopoly   415

HAMILTON RIVERS: Noon at Carl's Mainline Cafe   416

WAYNE V. NOYES, JR.: Front Porch Swing   418

JOYCE FENSTERMAKER: Sprinkler   419

IRA BRADFORD: Home from Work   420

LAUREL MADISON: Kids   422

GRADY SULLIVAN: Mourning Dove   423

JONI LEFEVRE: Bicycle Ride to the Cannery   424

WALTER INGRAM: In the Middle of the Middle West   425
HUGH WITT: Doorbell   426
KIRBY QUACKENBUSH: September Moon   428

Index of Subtitles   429
About the Author   439
Books by Dave Etter   441

There always was a relationship between poet and place. Placeless poetry, existing in the non-geography of ideas, is a modern invention and not a very fortunate one.

—Archibald MacLeish

A windmill, a junk heap, and a Rotarian in their American setting have more meaning to me than Notre Dame, the Parthenon, or the heroes of the ages. I understand them. I get them emotionally.

—Thomas Hart Benton

But I'm interested primarily in people, in man in conflict with himself, with his fellow man, or with his time and place, his environment.

—William Faulkner

I prefer men and women who live, breathe, talk, fight, make love, or go to the devil after the manner of human beings. Art is only valuable to me when it reflects humanity or at least human emotions.

—Edwin Arlington Robinson

In the end a man can expect to understand no land but his own.

—Vachel Lindsay

GEORGE MAXWELL
County Seat

Pushing deep into Sunflower County now,
just minutes before sunup,
the big semitrailer truck droning on
in the breezy, dew-heavy darkness;
leaving behind the cornfields,
the red barns, the windbreak trees,
snorting by the city limits sign
announcing ALLIANCE, pop. 6,428,
thumping across the railroad tracks
of the Chicago and North Western,
slipping past roadside produce stands
and hamburger and milkshake drive-ins,
bouncing and rattling again
between the bruised bodies of billboards
saying where to shop, eat, sleep,
where to fill up with gas:
LICHENWALNER'S DEPARTMENT STORE,
CARL'S MAINLINE CAFE,
HOTEL TALL CORN,
BOB'S TEXACO;
dipping toward the polluted waters
of the sluggish Ausagaunaskee River
and the once stately section of town
where neglected Victorian houses,
with their cupolas and wide porches,
are set back on maple-shaded lawns;
remembering good and bad times,
lost faces, half-forgotten names;
and then the driver taking a last drag
from his Marlboro cigarette,
poking me in the ribs
with yellow, tobacco-stained fingers,
one letter of Jesus on each knuckle,
breaking the long silence between us
by saying over the asthmatic breathing
of the great diesel engine
that we are here, this is it,
here's that town you've been asking for;
moving slowly into the Square,
with its domed and clocked courthouse,

1

its bandstand and Civil War monument,
its two-story brick buildings,
lawyers and doctors above,
the town's merchants below;
stopping on Main Street
next to the Farmers National Bank,
stepping down to the curb,
thanking the driver for the lift,
grabbing a U.S. Army duffel bag,
slamming the cab door with a loud bang,
then turning around to face
ALLIANCE CHAMBER OF COMMERCE
WELCOMES YOU
TO THE HYBRID CORN CAPITAL OF AMERICA,
and thus knowing for dead certain
that I'm back in the hometown
and that nothing has, nothing could have
really changed since I went away.

CHESTER GREENE
Taking the Census

Vines hold up the webby porch.
The birdbath hoards a dune of sand.
Broken toys bleed along a sagging fence.
But around in back
a Maytag washing machine
hums like a hive
and shirts are strung on a frayed line
that disappears in leaves.
I sit on the broken springs of an old car seat
and ask the usual questions.
Mrs. O'Toole folds red hands
over a watermelon belly
and tells me that nine sons are not enough.
I look about in horror.
The baby gives me a choice of worms.
I choose the one hanging out of his mouth.
Four boys are Indians.
They glare from their private tree.
The other four are cowboys.
None of them wear white hats.
The biggest boy asks me to join their game.
When I turn the invitation down flat,
an arrow gets me
right between the eyes.
I surrender quickly to both sides.
The gun barrel hurts my ribs.
Now, Mrs. O'Toole lies in the dust.
The cowboys have long ropes.
The redskins bring the fire.

HENRY LICHENWALNER
Living in the Middle

Here in Alliance, Illinois,
I'm living in the middle,
standing on the Courthouse lawn
in the middle of town,
in the middle of my life,
a self-confessed middlebrow,
a member of the middle class,
and of course Middle Western,
the middle, you see, the middle,
believing in the middle way,
standing here at midday
in the middle of the year,
breathing the farm-fragrant air
of Sunflower County,
in the true-blue middle
of middle America,
in the middle of my dreams.

ANDY HASSELGARD
Gone with the Grain

Wind whines the wine-colored telephone lines.

Girls who fool around grain elevators here
are always tucking in faded blue shirts,
two buttons unbuttoned from the top.

There are questions that will be asked:
"Who wrote my middle name on the water tank?"
"How many funny farmers in Farmer City?"

I don't care a whit what you say,
this is where I want to hang my hat.
Sure beats the park and the county courthouse.

The voices in the grand and grainy noon:
"Now I prefer an older-type woman myself."
"I used to had me a dog like him."

The girls glide around like graceful gazelles,
moving in and out of the dusty shadows.
I say howdy and then my tongue turns husk.

Wind whines the wine-colored telephone lines.

DOC MITCHELL
Windy

Brown leaves from the lightning-struck tree
blew down the sunbaked street.
The boy walked by the front porch
where I was shaking salt on a peeled egg.
He had a number eight on his tan T-shirt.
"Hey, Number Eight," I said,
"isn't this summer the windiest summer
we've ever had in Sunflower County?"
A strong swoosh of hot wind
rocked the bird-empty birdhouse.
The boy stopped, gave me a most serious look.
"I wouldn't be knowing that," he said.
"I've only been around for eight years
and my recall ain't so good yet."
I had to laugh, but it was the truth.
He hadn't noted the weather,
couldn't remember his first eight summers.
"Take care now, Number Eight," I said,
and I took a big bite of my salted egg
as the wind came on strong again.

ERNIE KEEPNEWS
Then and Now

There is a vacant blue frame house
down by the Burlington tracks
that Edward Hopper might have painted.

Aunt Bertha had an hourglass figure
right out of the Gay Nineties.

You can't make a snowball with slush.

Yellowing papers junk the front porch,
mostly the weekly shopping news,
which is free and not worth spit.

Beautiful Lillian Russell
weighed 180 pounds.

Slush is snow with the fun melted out.

A tiny hunchback lived in the house
and he liked to build snowmen
that were almost twice his size.

Why does the circus strong lady
always look so attractive to me?

Wish it would snow again, that's all.

WENDY OLSON
  Drought

We spent our
evenings of
that long and
sweltering
summer on
the front porch
too beat and
discouraged
to move to
damp beds and
dust fell from
the moon of
sleepless dreams
and one night
Lawrence Welk
played one of
those pukey
polka tunes
and Danny
stripped off his
boxer shorts
and went out
to the yard
and did a
nutty rain
dance in his
birthday suit
and Mama
yelled him back
with a rude
oath and smacked
his fanny
with a rolled
up copy
of Franklin's
Field and Stream
and it did
not rain for
nine weeks and
the soil cracked

and the corn
dried up and
choked to death
and spring calves
went hungry
as grass gave
out and hay
dwindled down
to almost
nothing and
my sick horse
*Galloping
Ghost* shot me
his mean look
and someone
in a Brooks
Brothers suit
on TV
from New York
said the drought
was not so
bad as we
all thought and
Daddy glared
at the man
and Grandma
looked at her
withered hands
and Grandpa
got out of
his chair and
threw his boot
at the screen
and the whole
world went dark.

MITCH VALENTINE
Billboard

The billboard is just plain tacky.
A hometown disgrace is what it is.
But as I stare at it today
from the weeds across the street,
a workman in bib overalls
finally gets a new bill in place.
Hooray, a circus is coming,
coming here to Sunflower County!
"We'll be there," I say to Prince,
who lifts his head and barks sharply.
Then we run home together,
down sun-dappled brick sidewalks,
so anxious to spread the news
to the other neighborhood dogs:
Lucas, Lion, Lobo, and Max.

WADE HOLLENBACH
Hard Cider

"Can I come too?" she said.
I said nothing and kept on walking,
moving away quickly down the railroad track.
But one-eyed Billie June came,
and she grabbed my hand and grinned.
Near the bridge we stopped and looked
at the moonlit waters
of the Ausagaunaskee River.
For a minute, I forgot she was with me,
lost as I was in my faraway thoughts,
my troubles in finding a new job.
"What's in the sack?"" she said.
I pulled out the tall dusty bottle.
"Hard cider?" she said.
"Hard cider," I said.
I screwed off the cap and took a long swallow.
"Can I have some?" she said.
I passed her the bottle.
She helped herself to three big gulps.
Her teeth were yellow, her dress was soiled,
and a hunk of coal-black hair
had fallen over her one good eye.
"Hard cider!" she said.
"Take it easy," I said,
"we've got the whole night ahead of us."
She kissed me smack on the lips,
knocking off my hat, dropping the bottle.
"Hard cider," I said,
and hurled a stone into the river.

APRIL McINTYRE
Fishing in the Rain

I left him there,
deep in his fishing,
six little trout,
their necks broken,
stuffed in the pockets
of his denim jacket,
the last worm waiting
in a coffee can,
cold rain pelting
the sycamore leaves.

I told him goodbye.
I had had quite enough
fishing in the rain.
He caught six trout
in the leafy cold.
I caught nothing.
Deep in his fishing,
he had one worm left.
It was his worm.
I left him there.

RED RADER
Electric Avenue

A woman in pink shorts was cutting up a tree
with the loudest chain saw in Sunflower County.
The sidewalk was covered with firecracker burns
and some chalked squares from a noisy hopscotch game.
Two boys wearing camouflage shirts and pants
sneaked in and out of bushes, firing toy guns.
From the porch steps of his stepmother's house
a college kid was blowing piss-poor trombone.
The tattooed man next door ran across the lawn
carrying a fish tank, the fish still in it,
and slammed it down on the stained and marked cement.
"Okay, let it begin right here," he screamed.
I watched from behind my snorting power mower,
trying to decide whether to smile or snicker.
"What's going to begin here?" my wife said.
It was then the rock hit the art-glass window.

BRIAN HARDY
Little Theater

They were casting
for William Inge's
Picnic tonight.
I went right over
and said I wanted
to be Hal Carter,
the guy who comes
to this Kansas town
and makes all the girls
go crazy with lust.
I told them
Picnic was my
favorite stage play
and I knew all the words
Hal Carter has to say
and that I was
just like Hal Carter.
They looked me
up and down
and shook their heads,
and I saw a smile
on the director's face.
He said, "Young man,
you're a bit too short
to play Hal.
Not husky enough.
Not enough big white teeth."
They told me
I could try out
for another role,
but I told them no.
I was Hal Carter
or nothing at all.
They said, "We're sorry.
We're awful sorry."
I left the theater
and walked out
into a pouring rain,
knowing I was stuck
with being me
for awhile longer.

14

I stopped for milk
and a cheeseburger
at the Spot-Lite Diner.
There was this girl
I like real good there.
I told her, "Holly,
you think you're hot stuff,
but you're not."
She was hurt and I'm glad.
William Inge, you can
write this down, too:
"Life ain't no picnic
for Brian Hardy."

OLIVER BRIGGS
Night Work

He got out of the car.
Got out his driver's license.
He said, "yes, sir,
no, sir, yes, sir."
He was polite as hell.
He was polite as hell.
He. was polite as hell.
Then his girlfriend
moves up to the car window
and shoots me in the shoulder.
A .38 Smith and Wesson.
Pulled it from her handbag.
"Take that, copper," she says.
Called me "copper."
Right out of a thirties movie.
"Take that, copper."
I went down of course.
Of course I went down.
Then he got back in the car
and they drove away.
Not burning rubber, not fast.
Like they had all night.
He was polite as hell.
He said "yes, sir,
no, sir, yes, sir."
Jesus, this night work
is going to kill me yet.

CHRISTOPHER MOORE
Lionel the Cat

My old white cat,
who digs hard bop,
plus all the new
stuff, is going
deaf. My wife blames
this on my loud
booming of the
stereo. "He
can't even hear
his own meow,"
she says. "Nonsense,"
I tell her, and
Lionel and
I go into
my den. "What are
you boys up to
now?" she says. "I
want Lionel
to pick up on
this fantastic
Dexter Gordon
album," I say.
"What's that again?"
she says, a hand
cupped to her ear.
"I love you and
Lionel loves
you too," I say,
and close the door.

LIZ ALTENBERGER
Rose Tattoo

It's no secret anymore.
I have a tattooed rose
on my upper left thigh.
It's a little pink rose
with a short green stem.
Rose petals on the ground.
Roses dying in the yard.
A rose is not a rose for long.
I wanted a rose
I couldn't lose.
I found out where
to go in Chicago,
where to get me a rose tattoo.
The electric needle
bit into my flesh.
Arrows of pain.
Trickles of blood.
The smell of disinfectant.
"You're next," the man said
to my flower-eyed girlfriend.
"I've changed my mind," she said.
"Fix you up in no time," he said.
"I don't think so," she said.
For weeks nobody
except my girlfriend
knew I had a rose on my leg.
With summer coming
I knew I couldn't keep
this secret much longer.
Last night I was in the shower.
Mom pulled back the curtain
and told me I had
an important phone call
about a job at Burger King.
She saw the pink rose,
couldn't take her eyes off it,
off my little tattoo,
all shiny with soap and water.
"We'll talk about this later,"
she said, and stared some more.

We talked about it for days,
about my ever-blooming,
ever-perfect rose.
"A tattoo is cheap," she said.
"Only cheap folks
go in for these cheap tattoos."
She must have forgotten
about Dad's blue anchor
from World War II,
high on his left arm.
"Tattoos are forever,"
my boyfriend said,
and kissed me on the thigh,
on my little rose tattoo.

BRUCE PUTNAM
Crayola

It was just a child's
crayon drawing,
but perfect somehow:
broad blue prairies
soaking in mist,
a lightning tree
still supporting
a rope swing,
and in the foreground
a bushy dog
asleep on a hill
of sycamore leaves.

"And where am I
in your picture?"
I asked her,
tugging a yellow braid.
"Oh, you're not here,"
she said, sadly.
"You've gone away
to Cincinnati,
dreaming of me
lost in a brick town
with too many weeds
and fences."

ELWOOD COLLINS
Summer of 1932

On sticky summer Sunday afternoons
there would be lots of people
standing around in the yard,
mostly relatives and neighbors
in cotton dresses and white shirts.
They would come and go until dusk,
talking, talking, talking, talking
about jobs, bread lines, foreclosures,
about Hoover and Roosevelt,
about the latest layoff or suicide.
Someone, usually my father
or one of my unemployed uncles,
would be scratching in the dirt
with half a hoe or ragged rake,
not to plant, not to cultivate,
but to be doing something, to be busy,
as if idleness was some kind of dark shame
or red pimple of embarrassment.
I was there, too, a silent child
with my blue wagon and blue spade,
making little mountains of dirt
and patting them down with my fist.
When the lemonade ran out,
my mother or a maiden aunt
would bring out a pitcher of water
and someone would always say,
"You can't beat good old water
when you have a terrible thirst."
The Ford in the driveway was ours.
It was leaking oil, drop by drop,
and the battery was dead.
We were obviously going nowhere.

LESTER RASMUSSEN
Jane's Blue Jeans

Hanging alone on a blue-rain clothesline,
hanging alone in a blue rain,
hanging alone:

a pair of torn blue jeans,
a pair of faded blue jeans,
a pair of Jane's blue jeans.

Blue jeans in the shape of Jane,
Jane now in another pair of blue jeans,
blue jeans that also take the shape of Jane.

Oh, Jane, my rainy blues blue-jeans girl,
blue jeans without you inside
is the saddest blue I've seen all day.

VALERIE MAYHEW
Cornfield Virgin

It was bad enough of you, Otis Riley,
to make that ruckus on the porch,
to swear and smash my new geranium pot
when I told you, "No, no, no,
you can't do that, no, never that."
But to stand there and repeat
over and over and over and over again
in that singsong voice of yours,
"Valerie Mayhew is a cornfield virgin,
Valerie Mayhew is a cornfield virgin,"
was the limit, the very limit.
The front room was loud with male talk,
thick with weather, politics, and crops,
so I think none of the men heard you.
But the kitchen window was open,
and my married aunts and pregnant cousins
who were drying supper dishes heard.
They heard. They heard it all.
Later, Mother, high on dandelion wine,
barged into the upstairs bathroom,
where I was soaking in a hot tub,
and said, in a blunt, loose-tongue way,
"Who's a virgin? Who's a virgin?
There's no son or daughter of mine
who's not been to the hayloft
at least once under the spell
of a spring moon or harvest itch."
So you've gone and done it, Otis.
Now when I talk about the wild boys
I went to college with down in Macomb,
the ones I parked in the weeds with,
they'll smile and their eyes will say,
"You're just a cornfield virgin, Val."

SHEENA FITZGERALD
   Pisces Sun

The pale Pisces sun has run out of blue sky
and fades again behind a cold cloud.
I see faces rising from the grave, saying
"I'll forgive you if you forgive me."
Memories of artichokes and lollipops,
grass-stained knees in a wind-rocked elm tree,
afternoons of Viennese waltzes that Mom
played on her small sickbed Victrola,
homework, "The Lone Ranger," an album of stamps.
I've saved a box of old valentines,
two dozen chipped marbles in a red string-bag,
a snapshot of Suzie Somebody.
The Mississippi of my blood keeps twisting
past the sandbars of a snarled childhood.
This knot in my belly could choke a father
who would bludgeon us with words or fists
and send us bawling to bed or out of sight.
My head is a zoo of warring tongues.
Is that the sulky sun coming out again
or a zodiac of suicides?

TANYA OWENS
Wrestler

They don't brag about me much
in Sunflower County,
but they love me
all over the Middle West.
And I mean places like
Des Moines, St. Louis,
Minneapolis,
Cleveland, Omaha,
Detroit, Milwaukee,
all them big towns.
There are no write-ups about me
in the local newspapers,
but when I step into the ring
to wrestle some tough broad
from Toledo or someplace
and the announcer says
to the crowd in the arena,
"In this corner,
from Alliance, Illinois,
weighing 196 pounds,
Tanya Owens,"
I know I'm somebody special
and flex my big muscles.
Then when the bell sounds,
I bang into my opponent
and throw her to the mat
and wear her down
with my strength and stamina,
then clamp on a body scissors
and use my huge thighs
to squeeze the life out of her
until she screams
"I give up. I give up."
My boyfriend, Biff,
talks me up proud
at Jim's barbershop.
"We're a matched pair," he says.
"We both weigh 196 pounds."

HATTIE EAKINS
V-J Day

It was V-J Day.
World War II was over at last
and the town was whooping it up
to beat the dickens.
It was a day to remember.
I'll not deny that.
I turned the radio on
after supper and a bath.
The station went from one city
to another city
and all you could hear
were loud and excited voices,
firecrackers, and car horns,
just like a summer New Year's Eve.
Ross was away on a business trip.
Had he been here he would have had
a strong drink or two
to celebrate this special date.
I thought at first
I would have a glass of red wine,
then decided on some good scotch.
I seldom touched the hard stuff,
but they were going crazy in Cleveland,
bonkers in Boston.
Next morning two cops
found me in the apple orchard,
still sleeping off my drunk.
I was naked as a jaybird,
having gone outside that night
without my nightgown on,
holding only the scotch.
Don't ask me what
I thought I was doing.
The wayward ways of drink are endless.
The cops got me to my feet,
wrapped a blanket around
my damp nakedness.
Soon all the men and boys
would be trooping home,

all the hometown heroes
of Alliance, Illinois,
all except our two sons
who wouldn't be coming home,
for the simple reason
that they never left,
one having shot himself in the left foot
against the hot breath
of the town's draft board,
and the other one
doing time in jail for being
a conscientious objector.
"It's a time to feel proud,"
the burly cop said.
"Yes, it is," the tall cop said.
"Sure, very proud," I said,
and bit my lower lip.

REX AGEE
Getting at the Truth

"There's more honest information
in a tomato can label
than in a week of newspapers,"
said Sherwood Anderson. So I
canceled the *Tribune*, the *Gazette*,
and the *Chronicle* and spent the
money on canned tomatoes. Then,
as the years skipped by, I forgot
about the *Tribune*, the *Gazette*,
and the *Chronicle*. My friends said
they were informed that I was the
smartest tomato can reader
in the entire Middle West. And
they never picked that news up from
any old newspaper, either.

LEE GUTHRIE
Country Smoke

Uncle Herbert is not here, I tell you.
No need for you to poke about the house.
I don't know what fickle prairie wind
swept him up and took him off somewhere.
Though he never said one way or the other,
he wasn't very happy here, I think,
what with my working at the lumberyard
and gone from near sunup to sundown.
Night after night I'd come home from work
to find him staring at the TV set,
like maybe it was a Vegas slot machine
about ready to vomit silver dollars.
Even after supper when the two of us
would leave the dishes and smoke by the stove,
he wouldn't say much, mostly nod his head,
grunt, clear his throat, or close his yellow eyes,
while I'd talk on and on and play the fool.
He's been gone now a fortnight or more.
I can't think of where he'd likely go.
He'd be pleased at your concern, I'm sure,
but I doubt if he'd find words to tell you so.
I'd be lying if I said I missed him.
A glum man like that ain't my first choice
for someone to have around the place,
let alone for a bed and board houseguest.
Uncle Herbert is not here, I tell you.

TUCKER STONE
Stuttering Hands

The broken-down barn of a man,
his face an Appalachia of ruts and gullies,
leans against the weathered bricks
of the Farmers National Bank.

It has quit raining again.
The high school boys coming up Main Street
break into a runaway gallop.
They are wild horses drunk in a green wind.

Approaching forty, I realize
that I am really terrified of growing old.
Already the buxom farm girls
are aware of my stuttering hands.

ORVILLE JUMP
Me, Myself, and I

The thin boy came out of the tall cornfield.
He had on blue jeans and a jean jacket.
I stared hard at his adolescent face.
Damn, this was me thirty-five years ago.
The same sandy hair, the same gray-green eyes.
But there were smears of blood on his right hand,
and his left hand held a bloody rabbit.
"Some animal got to him first," he said,
"and I finished him off with my jackknife."
A cold wind rustled the ragged cornstalks.
No, this wasn't me, this was never me.
Then I recalled the bird I stabbed to death,
the bluejay the cat caught when I was twelve.
"Bastard," I said, and punched him where he smiled.

MARY ANN CLEMENS
Sheet Music

After Sunday school
I raised the top of
the piano bench
and took out a stack
of sheet music I
hadn't seen for three
years and which my dead
mother used to play
on our old Baldwin,
especially "Red
Sails in the Sunset."
Daddy can also
play that tune, but when
I asked him to play
it again, he said
he had tried to play
it the other day
but couldn't see the
keys he was crying
so much. And I said
I understood and
put the sheet music
back where I found it
in the piano
bench, with "Red Sails in
the Sunset" on the
bottom of the stack,
under "Harbor Lights,"
and went into the
kitchen and made a
big fried-egg sandwich,
which I couldn't eat
and tossed out for the
birds who come around
and who can always
stomach anything
and go on singing.

ANGELA KNIGHT
Hot Rod

When these two boys whistled at me
from their loud and smoking car,
I was riding my bicycle.
The wicker basket in front
was crammed full of library books
and a box of Popsicles.
The boy at the wheel said,
"You want to go for a real ride?"
I kept moving right along River Street,
my bare legs pumping for home.
I didn't glance at either boy,
not after I saw them slow down
and knew what they were up to.
They drove beside me
and made a few more smart remarks,
mostly about my anatomy.
I turned into our driveway
and rang my bicycle bell at them,
once, twice, oh, four, five times.
My sister said that was real dumb.
Every day this week so far
these two boys have driven by here
and honked their horn and yelled,
"Hey, Angie, want to go for a spin?
How 'bout it, Angie baby?"
"Now don't get any ideas," Mom said,
and sighed heavily a couple of times.
"I had a car like that once," Dad said.
"I hated that car," Mom said.
"Yeah, but you rode in it," Dad said.
"Woo, woo," my sister said.
"Hey, Angie baby," my brother said.
"You're the right baby for me."
I don't think a little ride,
maybe around town and back,
would hurt any, do you?
If there's something that worries me,
it's that one day I'll ring my bell
and no one will notice,
no one will be there.

33

SUSAN COBB
Names

I want to be Susan Jonquil,
a bold springtime flower
sticking out of a jelly glass.
Or Susan Ferris Wheel.
Or Susan Television,
my bare tummy warm with loud pictures.
Or Susan Blueberry Muffin.
Or Susan Iuka, an Indian girl
sparkling in beads and silver rings.
But more than anything,
I want to be Susan Mississippi,
a river that does what it wants to,
and anytime it wants to,
moving south past fish and funny boats,
past moonlit towns and hooting owls.
And Susan Honeysuckle
would be summers of fun.
And so would Susan Lemonade
and Susan Lawnmower.
Look, I'm telling you right now,
being plain Susan Cobb
is no great thrill to me.

NICHOLAS HOBSON
Juney Love

She said she wasn't Juney Love,
but I said she was Juney Love.
When I squeezed her right knee,
she said if I wanted to touch her like that
I would have to change my name too.
"No problem," I told her,
and we walked hand in hand down the country road,
beyond a hollow stump filled with black water,
beyond the boarded-up schoolhouse,
beyond a worn-out sofa on a worn-out porch,
beyond three broken wine bottles.
Juney Love was very bold.
When we sat down in sticky weeds,
she pressed my hand against her sex
and then kept it there, kept it there.
"How would it be if we went somewhere
and I took off my clothes?" she said.
"Call me Sinbad," I said.

ROGER POWELL
The Talk at Rukenbrod's

I sit in the shade on the high curb
in front of Rukenbrod's grocery store.
I sip a cold Nehi Grape and listen to the talk:

"You remember Andy Gump, don't you?"

"My blue jeans are too tight, she tells me.
I feel creepy walking past the Square
with all those dirty eyes scraping my skin."

"No, I never knew Nettles. He was an Elk."

"Sure, Paul was farming in Pickaway County, Ohio,
but he got going in this spiritualism stuff.
Goes all over now. West Coast and all."

"Butterflies, you know, taste with their feet."

"The wife took the kids down to Hannibal,
Mark Twain's hometown on the Mississippi.
I told her to bring me back a nice souvenir."

"Joe Palooka I remember. My brother Jake liked him."

"Nettles ran a forklift up at the cannery.
Then he was with A&W Root Beer, nights.
Heart attack it was. In Terre Haute, I heard."

"A purple martin eats 2,000 insects per day."

"So I think I got me a modest daughter, see.
But last week I catch her with another girl.
And they weren't playing no dominoes, neither."

"Fred's cousin was formerly with Dial-a-Prayer."

"Guess what they brought me from Hannibal?
A Becky Thatcher back scratcher! No lie.
I didn't know whether to laugh or throw a fit."

36

"Butterflies do what? Taste with their what?"

I take my empty into Rukenbrod's grocery store.
·They have run out of Nehi Grape.
I grab a Dr. Pepper and sit down again.

"You sure you don't remember Andy Gump?"

FLORA RUTHERFORD
Postcard to Florida

What brightens up this prairie town in spring?
Not tulip, not dandelion, not willow leaf,
but New Holland, Massey Ferguson, and John Deere.
Right, the brand-new farm equipment
glistening now in the rooster-strutting sun.
And oh what colors they have given us:
strawberry red, sweet-corn yellow, pie-apple green.
A fragrant breeze drifts in from the plowed earth.
The excitement of crops seeds my furrowed brain.
Mother, we have come through another wintertime
and I had to write and tell you this.

HENRY KRENCHICKI
Tallgrass Township

Bogged in dog days once more,
my restless daughters
fidget and fuss indoors,
then drift out to the lawn,
with its patches of shade.
My uncle Christopher is there,
under a big oak tree,
painting five yellow boxcars
of the Cadiz Railroad
on a piece of canvas.
He once drove a truck
in McLean County
for Illinois Biscuit Company,
but won't talk of that now,
being too busy with paint.
The mailman brings the mail
and we say hello.
A letter from St. Louis
tells me that all is well
with David and Barbara Clewell.
Also that Mr. Charlie
and his sidekick Ollie
have secured the back door
to their Pershing Street flat.
In white-hot bathing suits,
my daughters drive away
in a Ford pickup,
gone to the public pool
in the public park.
It's too humid to do much,
not that I could do more
if it were cold as Christmas.
Yes, I'm flat broke again,
stuck in this dull town,
in this torpid township.
Seems I'm always the next in line
when the Ferris wheel
breaks down at the fair.

DAWN CASAGRANDE
Concert

Until the cops came
and took him away,
there was a bearded stranger
in a black and white checked suit
playing the harmonica
on the sidewalk in front
of our defunct opera house.
He had attracted a small crowd
of Saturday shoppers
and a few old men
who wandered over
from the clean green benches
on the Courthouse lawn.
The cops were gentle but firm.
No one said anything
in the way of protest,
except lame Johnny Johncock,
who asked if the man
could maybe stick around
a wee bit longer
so he could play his
"Roses of Picardy" again.

LUKE HENNESSEY
Time Clock

With Friday paychecks
in wallet, purse, and pocket,
we line up at the time clock.
The work week is almost over.
The big smiles are back.
A usually silent man
chatters away like a bluejay.
A black woman swings her hips
in a provocative dance.
Anything said or done
even slightly funny
brings raucous laughter.
Oh what old jokes and one-liners,
what nudgings and shakings,
what tired but happy faces.
We grip our named and numbered cards,
passports to the carefree weekend,
in our work-toughened fingers.
At last, the time clock
blinks to three-thirty.
We drop the cards into the slot,
whisk them out again,
and slip them into the rack.
The line moves ahead, grows shorter.
My turn comes and I punch out
and slam through the wide side door.
The parking lot is full of snow.
I walk over to my car,
start up the engine,
then scrape the windshield clean.
Brothers and sisters
of the long warehouse week,
comrades of conveyor belt,
lunchroom, and time clock,
we're going home again.
And isn't it about time?

STANLEY ADAMS
County Road K

I said: "Slow down. Good lord, man, this road
ain't no interstate highway, you know.
Look at the damn dust you're raisin' up."

He said: "So what. The gravel and junk
shoots behind us. We're not gettin' none.
I always drive fast, no matter what."

I said: "Sure thing. But if one big stone
jumps up and cracks a headlight, you'll quit.
You just ain't usin' no common sense."

He said: "Shit, Stan. No need to sweat blood.
We hit blacktop again past that farm.
Sit back, stay cool, and enjoy the view."

42

WILLIAM GOODENOW
The Red Depot

Morning fog engulfs the red depot.
I move up closer and smell coal smoke.
There are phantoms on the brick platform,
ghosts that rode a lot of varnish.
Sherwood Anderson paces in his floppy felt hat.
Vachel Lindsay scribbles on an old envelope.
Carl Sandburg puffs a stub cigar.
Can I believe this? Can I?
Suddenly very excited, I take a look around.
A baggage wagon is loaded with sacks of mail.
Eight bankers check giant gold watches.
The stationmaster sells a ticket to Topeka.
Beyond the water tower a whistle wails.
Blue rails begin to hum.
Hey, that's it, that's the good music.
Eagerly, expectantly, I stare down the tracks.
The *Corn Belt Limited* will be right on time.
But I wait and wait and still no train comes.
Something's wrong. Something is terribly wrong.
Now the sun sucks the fog away.
I am standing in a new parking lot.
The red depot is a long-lost memory.
All the steam locomotives are gone to scrap.
Most of the engineers and firemen are dead.
No one's there to holler "Allllll aboard!"

JAMIE McFEE
Big Sister

Patty's legs, the bruises a deep purple,
were hanging out of the windy tree.
I wanted to talk to her face
but it was hidden in the dancing leaves.
This was the time of her first trouble,
her walking around seeing none of us,
even falling down the cellar stairs.
Now she was up there in the carved maple
sucking hard on something juicy.
I didn't know what it was, but juice drips
would come down wetting my hot cheeks.
My neck was beginning to cramp a bit,
with my head poked up that way,
looking into the sister-hiding tree.
I couldn't get up there, couldn't make
that first big branch to swing a leg over,
though I had tried and tried hard,
wanting to keep up with her if I could.
I had my radio on the music
and it was twanging in my good ear.
Patty was still eating something runny
and yelled for me to turn down the sound.
"You know that song makes me sad," she said.
She was always, always saying that,
even crying suddenly at supper table,
remembering what was unhappy someplace.
I slid around the tree trunk a little,
hoping to get a better look at her.
The music was banging in my skull,
wilder than wild rain or tornado winds,
a dozen overheated guitars going crazy.
Then a strong wind came swooshing in,
and her dress blew up with the leaves.
There was a blood-red spot on her panties,
and maybe this was part of her trouble.
My neck was hurting more and my back too.
It was no fun standing there,
seeing purple legs but not Patty's face,
and she not caring to play a game

or ride bikes or roll on the grass,
though I asked her to and begged her to.
So I turned up the radio on the music
until it was as loud as it would go,
and walked through the flower beds,
kicking at all the blood-red tulip faces,
wondering if it was a good thing
to grow up and be grown up
and not like anything anymore.

SAL BIVIANO
Pennies

It was 1935, you know,
and I remember one time
coming home from grade school
when we boys put pennies
on the railroad tracks
so *The Empire Builder*
could make our coins bigger coins.
Jackie Lee put a nickel on
and walked home with an eye
that would soon turn black.
Show-offs need not apply
to the Garfield Street gang
in those flat-busted days.
It was 1935, you know.

MELISSA JENKINS
Staring into Winter

Big flakes of snow
fall on the last remaining oak tree leaves.
I love the dry, ticking sound they make
on this storm threatening afternoon.
There should be an owl somewhere nearby,
tightening his feathers and staring into winter.
I know there are deer about,
for I have seen two of them cross the road
day before yesterday,
just up past the railroad tracks.
And where is the red fox
that jumped the barbed wire last spring,
hightailing it out of Ruby Cooper's chicken yard?
Snow in big flakes
thickens in the scrap of oak woods on the hill.
I have an empty house to go to
and cold thoughts to rattle in my head.
Pray for me, Father,
and for the deer whose gentle eyes
are the color of syrup bubbling in the pan.

YVONNE WYNCOOP
   Looking at Clouds

I am looking at black rain clouds
and a patch of bright blue sky
the exact shape of Illinois,
a state where my crazy aunt Minnie
spent her whole life saying,
"Aren't we ever going to move from here?"
Look, the patch of sky is looking
very much now like Delaware,
a state my aunt never heard of.
And a good thing, too, since that's
a place with all those historic houses
and first families with family trees
rooted among the dank bogs of England.
No, she would have never shut up
had she known about Delaware
and the thin green mists they have there,
her bony finger tracing the map
eastward out of Sunflower County.

FRANK TEMPLE
Wet Spring, Dark Earth

Hope

Wasting away in her bed of psalms,
my mother opens tired eyes to say,
"I'll be on my feet in a week or two."

Agony

She will have no doctors, no drugs.
The Lord is her shepherd, her trust.
But His rod, His staff don't comfort me.

Death

Here on April's tulip-trembling hill
the gravestones darken in the thin rain.
We stop at a fresh grave, a new stone.

Love

Sister Betsy, seven years old in May,
shows me her buggy of sleeping dolls.
"Every one of them is a mama," she says.

Memory

My father stands under a fragile moon,
pounding cold fist into cold hand,
his Donna dying in a gospeled room.

Faith

Deep in a green-bladed field of corn
I pray I may honor my mother's faith,
and know that in God there is no death.

DANIEL KORNBLUM
Bad News

The first day in the sixth grade
we had to tell about how
we spent our summer vacation.
I didn't want to tell a thing,
but I did and I said,
"Lots of good things almost happened
and lots of bad things did."
Miss Woodley said didn't I want
to say a little more than that,
and I said all right, all right,
but nobody's going to like it,
and she said, "Go on, Daniel,"
and I stood by the side of my desk and said,
"We were going to go to Alpine, Texas,
to see my sick grandmother
who was close to a hundred,
but she died of heart failure,
then we were going to go to Hollywood
to see my older brother, Jim,
but he joined a religious cult
with this dumb friend of his,
then we were going to go to Ohio
to see my uncle Victor
who was laid off at the steel mill
and drinking too much gin and stuff,
but he killed himself with a gun,
and then we were going—"
"That will be enough," she said.
"You can sit down now, Daniel,"
and I sat down and was glad
I didn't have to go over
all that misery again.

ROY ORSULAK
An Ordinary Sinner

What are we going to do, you know so damn much?

Threw rocks at all six streetlights
over on Kansas Street
which stayed dark for three whole nights.
Rocks, rocks, rocks, and more rocks
busted up all the streetlights.
And we never got caught.

I'm confused, it being an element of my nature.
Plus my nature also contains plenty of fear
when I'm with someone who has shot a cow.

Booted my birthday football
and smashed a statue in Reverend Garwood's yard:
the long yard,
the wrong yard,
the sad yard,
the bad yard.

What you better do as quick as you can
is to hop aboard that freight train
and say you work for the Burlington Railroad.

Forged Mother's name on ten-dollar check.
Went downtown to cash it,
and did cash it, and did cash it
at Rukenbrod's grocery store.
Then they called Mother up.
Goodbye ten bucks, hello Father's belt.

Run, boy, your fat is on the fire.

MOLLY DUNAWAY
Rainbow

When I get good and mad at my man
I take off my engagement ring
and put it in the empty Rainbo bread wrapper
that I keep under the bed
or slung away on a top closet shelf.
Red and blue and oodles of yellow:
such a happy wrapper to wrap bread in,
but much too gay and giddy
for an off again on again diamond ring.
Then I'll watch a mushy movie on TV
and get choked up at the love scenes
and run upstairs and get out my ring,
safe and secure in its bread wrapper.
Today it rained and we had a rainbow,
all candy pink and watery gold.
I didn't wear my man's ring all day.
Rainbo bread, slices of the well-fed dream.
My bright dreams of love, of loving him.
Are they real as Rainbo bread?
Or only fast-fading rainbow dreams?

ZACHARY GRANT
Guilt

We drive to Chicago's Union Station.
I say goodbye, give her a quick kiss.
My Nancy Lee is going off to New Hampshire.
We never got along. I'm glad she's gone.
But then, back home again, it hits me.
I saw only her faults, her blemishes.
After brooding over a few whiskey sours,
I stumble around in a blues funk.
The neighbors put away their porch swing.
A truck dumps coal at the fuel company.
Sad and alone in October's smoky twilight,
I walk through the black walnut trees.
Across the broken limestone wall, I see
rusty soup cans, a discarded water heater.
A squirrel scampers among dry leaves.
The empty birdhouse darkens on its pole.
Far off, a freight train blows for a crossing.
The wind turns cold. I think of snow.
Well, there's not much more I can say.
I was always right. Now I'm wrong.
I know it's no picnic being a father,
but if you have an ugly-ducking daughter,
close your eyes and love her to death.

NEIL CAMPBELL
Humor

My long-time buddy Humpy Walls,
a hunchback who writes the sports news
for our own *Alliance Gazette,*
has a priceless sense of humor.
Take this afternoon, for instance.
We're coming out of the Elite,
after cherry pie and coffee,
when we bump into Bert Foster,
who works at Guthrie's Feed and Grain,
and who says, his face close to Hump's,
"Hey, Walls, it's been damn near two years.
Where's the seven bucks you owe me?"
Humpy just grins his grin, then says,
"Don't you worry, Bert, you'll get it
when I get myself straightened up."

STUBBY PAYNE
Stocking Tops

In June the syringa bushes bloom,
and I swear that I can smell oranges there.
That was your smell, Bee. I knew it well.

And I think of you today in Arne's Pub,
where all winter long you sipped Gordon's gin,
legs crossed, showing a bulge of creamy thigh
above those tantalizing stocking tops.

Green summer again. Rain. The warm earth steams.

You left town on a Burlington day coach
to visit an aunt in Prairie du Chein.
"She's full of money," you said, "and dying of cancer."

Toward the end of July,
Sunflower County cornfields turn blond.
Stiff tassels shake in the sexual sun.
There's a dust of pollen in the air.

How many bags of potato chips?
How many trips to the can?
Oh, how many quarters in the jukebox, Bee?

August heat. The girls go almost naked here.

Like some overworked Cinderella,
you always took off just before midnight
on the arm of Prince or Joe or Hal or Smith,
bound for your place above the shoe store.

Yes, I should have bedded down with you myself,
said so what if you were a bumbling barfly,
every drinking man's little honey bush.

AMBER WHEATLEY
Out to Lunch

A bad morning and now
one more frustration.
The sign in the window
at Ludwig's jewelry store
says OUT TO LUNCH
and the bent hands
of the cardboard clock
are set at 2:15,
when, hopefully, he'll be back.
Ludwig is always, always
out to lunch, it seems,
or gone fishing,
or just not there.
Yes, I'll return
and try to keep my cool,
but he better have my watch
ticking on time again.
I don't much care
what day it is,
but to not have the time
strapped to my wrist
makes me jumpy and cross.
Is life getting me down?
Let me count the ways.

FORREST DAY
   Reds

The leaves of our ancient pear tree,
whose trunk is split, partly rotted,
have turned red-orange, flutter in cold wind.

A whole farmyard of autumn reds:
red horse, red combine, red chicken, red barn.

Scarlet windfall apples brighten pale grass.

The last of the garden tomatoes,
ones that never ripened to red, left there,
are now white-cheeked, mushy,   frost-killed.

Ruby-red ear of Indian corn.

Pine cones in late afternoon's crimson light:
craggy faces of tenant farmers.

Chopping firewood, I nick a careless thumb,
go inside to stop the bleeding,
heat up a plate of red-flannel hash.

MADELINE KUCHARIK
Devotion

It was just the two of
us, Father and me, in
that lonely house at the
edge of town, and I would
wait on him, hand and foot,
for it was his love I
wanted and he knew there
was no one else in my
life and that he could count
on his girl Madeline
to do things for him, day
or night, and I always
did what he told me to
as soon as possible
and not put him off, so
when he would tell me, "Go
down to the market and
bring back some grapefruit juice,
a half pound of bacon,
two dozen eggs, and some
bananas," or "Iron this
shirt right now because I
must be out of here in
seven minutes," I dropped
what I was doing and
got to the task at hand,
and even though his thank
yous came seldom, I knew
he was grateful and loved
me in his own strange way
and I was satisfied,
and then he died last year
and I had no one to
do things for and would pace
the silent rooms of that
big old house till I could
stand it no more and slashed
my wrists with a bread knife
and then got scared when I

58

saw all the blood and ran
into the street where this
lady friend of Father's
stopped her automobile
and said, "You stupid fool,"
and pushed me into the
back seat and drove to the
hospital, and later
I heard her tell the nurse,
"She's always been spoiled and
selfish and never cared
for no one but herself,
and it's no small wonder
she's never been married."

JESSIE LONDON
Keeping On

Last winter we lost Father.
Then in April we lost Mother.
But, look, we're doing all right.
We have a new Zenith TV
and I had a Franklin stove put in.
An old friend from school days,
who will write but won't visit,
wonders why I say "we,"
when "Aren't you all alone now?"
Some folks just don't know too much.
I have six cats boarding here,
plus my old dog, Mister Johnson,
named for the English writer,
not for Lyndon the president,
and this morning I was down
at the pet store looking over
a myna bird, a white mouse,
and two rabbits that look like fun.
If I'm "alone," how come the kitchen
is so crowded at meal time?

VERONICA BROOKS
Jogging

I jog along Willow Creek Road.
It is corn-planting time again,
the last killing frost ten days gone.
Aunt Grace's funeral yesterday.
The open casket, white tulips,
the slow ride to the cemetery.
My right thigh stiffens up a bit.
I go over and sit down for a minute
on the stone step of the pioneer church,
its narrow stained-glass window
jeweled with afternoon light.
Aunt Grace's powdered face, for our eyes only.
It begins to rain, just a sprinkle.
The sweet smell of new grass
and the dark aroma of plowed ground
quicken me as never before.
I massage my sore thigh muscle
and think about jogging some more.
Aunt Grace never liked my body building,
my lifting barbells in a gym.
She lived on a big farm nearby,
over by the town of Noon Prairie.
She baked a ton of apple pies
and canned every green bean in sight.
I'm about two miles from Main Street.
My legs ache but I won't quit now.
I'll never forget the time Aunt Grace
blew up a monumental storm
when word got out that I had won
a wet T-shirt contest at Arne's Pub.
"Say something, Ed," she said.
"Too late now," Dad said, and smiled
and put his pipe back in his mouth.
Warm weather is here at last.
The corn crop will soon grow tall.
This is what I love to do, to jog
and feel the sweat run down between my breasts
and know that what I do is Veronica.

SISSY RICHARDSON
Bubble Gum

See the skinny girl with stringy hair.
Bigger, bigger, bigger, bigger,
an enormous gum-pink bubble,
then *pop, splat,* will you look at that,
a pink mask over her pink and chewing face.

Pink hat, pink dress, pink shoes.
She's all dressed up for Easter Sunday.
But dressed, too, in bubble gum.
Pink, pink, pink, getting pinker.

We never liked her at all.
Now we laugh, for she's one of us,
one of us bubble gummers.

The larger the bubble, the more the trouble.
Trouble in pink, sticky Easter pink.

Bubble gum, we chew you madly.

NINA JAMES
Writing Down the Dream

Courthouse clock bonging in my window.
Bedroom shaped like a loaf of french bread.
On the floor, red lace panties, red lace bra.
Thin blue shaft of frosty moonlight.
Walking out of the house with nothing on.
V of geese flying over packing plant.
Trolley car stops and I ride to cornfields.
Li'l Abner sipping a brown bottle of 3.2 beer.
Horse thief hanging from a horse barn hook.
My breasts swinging when I ran away.
Loud litanies and booming burial psalms.
Pioneers rising from pioneer graves.
Then I'm up in a tall cedar tree.
I'm eating penny candy, my jawbreaker going white.
Papa calling, "Get down, get down at once."
Pulls me by the ear into steamy kitchen.
Mama in saddle shoes frying eggs and bacon.
Zenith radio playing big band songs.
"Green Eyes," "One Dozen Roses," "Elmer's Tune."
Pink paper moon at our graduation dance.
Glenn Miller waving a golden trombone.
Now I'm at an afternoon double-feature movie.
Newsreel is full of soldiers and DC-3s.
Bombs falling on England, London on fire.
Returning home past a four-silo farm.
Bales of straw stacked against frame house.
Split-rail fence around an abandoned church.
Scarecrow, head resting on a hymnal.
Old Plank Road and Old Plank Bridge.
Something bulky down there in the river.
Body of biology teacher with snakes for hair.
Suddenly it grows dark, super dark.
Glare of steam locomotive's one-eyed stare.
I screamed, I screamed, didn't I?

GABE INGELS
Jazz Night

I had five friends of mine
from Du Page County
over to the house last weekend
to hear some new jazz
and play some jazz of our own.
It was a historic powwow,
one for the calendar.
It was the night we made
the soprano saxophone
the Illinois state instrument.
There was little discord.
It was done with real class.
Some of us were gentle.
Some of us were cool.
For those wanting the score,
the soprano sax got three votes,
the flugelhorn two,
the bass clarinet one.
With that out of the way,
we took bottles of Bass ale
to the dewy front yard
and watched the blowing moon
drop some golden notes.
"Well, somebody had to do it,"
I said, lighting my pipe.
"You're right," Hal Clancy said.
"I'll let the governor
know in the morning,
and the newspapers
and TV stations too."

DARLENE WINTERS
Funeral Home

I knew nothing about death.
Skippy Holliday lived down the block.
His dad was an undertaker.
One afternoon after church
we went to the funeral home basement,
took off our shoes and stockings,
and climbed into the caskets.
"What a peachy place
to play hide and seek," I said.
I laid on my back in a child's coffin,
all cushy with white satin,
and closed my eyes tight.
Skippy shut the lid on me.
"You're dead, Darlene," he said.
"You'll be in Heaven soon now."
Then, laughing, he let me out of there.
Next thing we did was to stretch out
in a large metal casket
that had shiny brass handles.
"We're both dead this time," he said.
"You were eaten by an alligator.
I fell off a mountain peak."
Skippy walked his clammy fingers
under my Sunday skirt.
"The dead don't tickle," I said.
Finally, the caskets were no more fun
and we went outdoors
with a box of Ritz crackers
and glasses of strawberry Kool-Aid.
I knew nothing about death.

HORACE LOVEJOY
Abraham Lincoln

History
has it that in
1858
Abraham Lincoln
came to visit
a cousin
in Alliance, Illinois.
The cousin,
whose name nobody
seems to know,
said to Abe,
"There are many
citizens here
in Sunflower County
dying to meet you."
After a noon meal
of ham, hominy,
and buttermilk biscuits,
the cousin
and Mr. Lincoln
went downtown,
such as our downtown
was in those days,
and Lincoln
shook hands with
the blacksmith,
the grain dealer,
one banker,
two young lawyers,
an old doctor,
several babies,
four dogs, two cats,
and everyone
he could find
on Main Street,
not excluding
the members
of a local group
that called themselves
Lincoln True Hearts.

Honest Abe said,
"This is a fine town
and you are
mighty fine folks.
Will you vote for me?"
Everyone nodded
their heads yes,
including
the dogs and cats,
and a red-faced lady
with a sunbonnet
stuck on her head
told the Rail Splitter
to whip the piss
out of that scoundrel
Stevie Douglas.
Abraham Lincoln
then said goodbye to
his cousin
and got aboard
a steam train
and left town
and kept on
shaking hands
and running for
high political office
until he became
history.

MELVIN TIKOO
Rocking

I mowed the front-yard grass,
I mowed the side-yard grass,
I mowed the back-yard grass,
then I sat in the rocking chair
on the shady screened porch.
I called in through the screen door,
"I want a sexy woman,
a pretty little puss
to sit right here on my lap."
My wife came out of the house,
pink curlers in her clean hair,
and she sat on my lap,
and we rocked in the rocking chair.
We rocked and rocked and rocked
in the rocking rocking chair.
"Time we ate supper," she said.
"Okay," I said. "Okay."
And I emptied the cut grass
from the wet cuffs of my pants
and went inside with my wife.

LONNIE EVANS
Diminuendo in Green

It began in the spring of the year,
the year I left school for good.
I fell in love with the color green.
I wanted green things,
the world's good green things.
I bought green shirts and pants.
I wore green socks
and a green baseball cap.
I even grew fond of green beans
and green sports cars.
I drew pictures of green frogs and snakes
and green bananas hanging from trees.
At the town pool or in the park
I looked for girls with green eyes.
When it rained it rained green rain.
I sat on the porch in a green chair
and watched green leaves.
This led me to green books.
I read Joyce and Robert Frost.
They wrote green books.
I read *How Green Was My Valley*,
"The force that through the green fuse
drives the flower," then searched out
green legends and green myths.
I went on greening for a spell,
lost in green thoughts.
Then the grass burned brown.
Yes, the grass turned brown.
I fell in love with the color blue.
Look, blue was all we had
in that drought-troubled town.
Blue opened my eyes.
Blue was cloudless skies.
That fall I gave my brother Buck
my green suede shoes.
He never thanked me at all.

PATRICK HANIFAN
Scarecrow

Drinking whiskey in the moonlight
on a hot night in late summer,
walking out of town on railroad ties,
past water tower and city dump,
I stopped to take another drink,
then walked on through the thick and sticky air.
In a moon-drenched cornfield,
Scarecrow was waiting for me.
He grabbed me by my shirt, took the bottle,
and spun me dizzy in the dirt.
"Scarecrow," I said, "you got no right—"
"When a man needs a drink real bad,
he's got the right," Scarecrow said,
and he drained the whiskey to the final drop,
then dropped the bottle at my feet
and turned his glance away from mine.
I watched him there for a spell.
Moonshine horselaughed his scarecrow face.

WAT NUGENT
Epitaph

I was born a bastard in a pickup truck
between two corn towns south of here
and wrapped in a sack the dog peed on.

I was always puny for my age,
never fast in school or first at sports,
quick to get lost and muddy.

I was born for cold, windy fields,
long hours behind the barn,
and machinery that wouldn't work.

I was dropped on my head at two,
crippled by a horse at twelve,
shot by a cracked duck hunter at twenty.

I was born to die piece by piece
and looked to death for a better life,
for life not death was the death of me.

SHERMAN CARTER
Bikinis

Got out of bed
last Saturday
morning with a
bad hangover
and went downstairs
for some grapefruit
juice, rye toast, and
coffee and made
another vow
not to stay up
late with drinking
friends and down so
many highballs,
when the back door
opened and my
sixteen-year-old
daughter, Daisy,
came in, followed
by eight or nine
other girls in
bikinis who
all glistened with
suntan oil, and
my daughter said
it sure is hot
and steamy out
there, and I stared
at a blonde girl
who was giving
a strawberry
cone a real fine
licking with her
little pink tongue
while sweat ran down
between large breasts
and I said it
is starting to
get rather warm
and steamy in
here too, and the

girls all giggled
and took soft drinks
out to the lawn
and then rubbed some
more suntan oil
on their lovely
arms and legs and
stretched out on big
bath towels, and
I went up to
the window and
snatched a good look,
then sighed and went
upstairs for a
long cold shower.

AMOS BLACKBURN
War of the Hybrids

Who has conquered these Midwestern cornfields?

Pioneer
Northrup King
Stewart
Dairyland
Pride
Lynks
DeKalb
Cargill
O's Gold
Acco
Funk's G-Hybrid
Hughes
Jacques
P-A-G
McNair
Trojan
Big D
Super Crost
Hulting
Bo-Jac

See their proud signs in the September sun.

DIANE GUBICZA
Spanish Peanuts

I didn't want to baby-sit some more,
so got a job at J.C. Penney,
which consisted mostly of weighing nuts
and selling candy, not excluding
Squirmy Worms, Atomic Fireballs,
Gummi Bears, Root Beer Barrels,
Pixy Stix, and Licorice Bites.
The first afternoon I was there
Carney Fisher comes in
and we get into a big fight
about my leaving him and going off
with Richie Gardner at Paula's picnic.
His voice got louder and louder.
I told him, "Leave me alone.
Can't you see I'm working?"
But he wouldn't go away.
He was waving his arms about
and banging his fist on the counter.
I told him, "Never speak to me again."
Then he calmed down somewhat
and had me weigh him a half pound
of those little Spanish peanuts.
He ate a handful or two,
licking the salt off his fingers.
"Don't ever see Richie Gardner no more.
Never. You hear me?" he said.
I told him, "I will if I want to."
He got terribly red in the face
and dumped the peanuts over my head.
People were stopping to stare at us.
Someone must have gone for Mr. Rooney,
'cause in a few minutes he comes up
and tells me I am fired.
Boy, that Carney Fisher fixed me good.
I want to save to buy a car.
You can't do that baby-sitting.
I've had it with changing diapers,
wiping noses, playing part-time mother.

ELEANOR ASHBY
Thinking of Cancer

The tree surgeons
come in a white
truck and saw down
the half-dead elm.
After they leave
I stroll across
the street and put
my outstretched hand
on the pale stump.
The fevered flesh
begins to cool.
All day, all night
I feel funny.
I roam my chest,
my throat for lumps,
wonder why my
hip hurts, my leg.
Amputation,
a deadly fact.
Mortality
gnaws on old bones.
The elms are sick.
Let's choose our trees.
I'll be maple.

MATT ROLLINS
A Chicago Romance

We met at a spin-the-bottle party.
She was a dark and curly sixteen,
a fun-loving high school dropout.
I was twenty-one, a wage slave
loading trucks five nights a week
at Marshall Field's warehouse
over on Harrison Street.
We were crazy in love, real gone
as the forties swingers would have it.
Her parents worked day shifts,
so we had lots of time to play
before I had to tell her goodbye
and take the elevated to work.
Boy, she was a hot number.
She'd climb all over me until
I was out of my mind with lust.
I told her one day, "Hey, look here,
this is my chair and that is your chair.
Now stay there, lover girl,
and let me catch my breath."
This romance ran clear off the rails
after just two months and two days
when her mother, in a tizzy,
said we couldn't see each other,
not tomorrow, not for a long time.
She told me Gwenda was too young
to get serious with a man,
had to get herself back to school,
back to reality, back to sense.
Her moustached father said nothing,
but looked at me from the doorway
with his postman's canceled-stamp frown.
I still feel the feel of her
and smell the smell of her.
What pains me, what really hurts,
is that she'd be only fifty-four now.

CAROL PARMALEE
Foreclosure

It wasn't
the stony-eyed
humiliation
of watching our
farm equipment
and the furniture
and appliances
being auctioned off
in the yard
that got to me,
but the dark
knowing that when all
the dusty cars
and pickups
pulled out into
the broken sunset
that our family
would no longer
be calling
the farm our home.
Now that's what hurt
and still hurts.
That and the fact
that if we failed,
how was it we failed
when for so long
we didn't fail
and kept going
and kept trying
to do better,
through good years
and bad years?
The farmer
who hangs himself
in the barn,
the wife who
sinks into silence
over her sewing
when it's certain

the last small hope
is crushed for good
is not for us.
We don't want
to come up short
again so soon.
But now, miles
and miles away,
under a new roof
with relatives
none too happy
to have us here,
I sometimes
get so darn blue
and depressed
I think for sure
I can't get up
for another day.
This cold world can
bust your heart
anytime,
anywhere.
It can hand you
your Sunday hat
and show you
to the nearest door
before you
can barely
believe your eyes.

JUSTIN UHLENHAKE
Tickets

Seriously,
I'm tired of tearing
tickets in half
at the Paradise theater
and keep thinking
of my Melba and me
at the carnival
last summer when we
walked in a soft rain
between the Ferris wheel
and the Tilt-a-Whirl,
and she said, "Justin,
I'm going to join
the Peace Corps next week,"
and she did it
and she's over there
in Africa now,
and I'm stuck right here
in Alliance, Illinois,
standing in the lobby
of this old movie house
in my frayed uniform,
taking tickets
for a stupid
Charton Heston film
and wondering why
Melba's letters
are so short and far apart,
and worrying that
I'm losing her love
and that I must do
something important,
like studying to be
a chiropractor
or driving a UPS truck,
so that she will
once again take me
seriously.

CLARENCE FOWLER
Nuts and Bolts

Now what's a *Farm Journal* doing in a doctor's office?

Look, if I could only point to a tractor
out in someone's cornfield or in the barnyard
and announce with an authoritative voice,
"Say, there's a Massey-Ferguson 1130:
Perkins direct-injection diesel engine,
turbocharged 120 horsepower,
hydrostatic-power-steering,
air conditioned cab, air-luxe seat, etcetera,"
it just might make my mechanically-minded son
sit up and take another glance at his old man.

Think hard: Do I know a nut from a bolt?

And then if I could go on to proclaim,
ever so casually, you understand,
"Hey, take a gander, will you, at the brand-new
New Holland 1469 haybine mower-conditioner:
37 horses, water-cooled engine,
and a sickle bar that can cut hay
at 1,520 strokes per minute,"
the boy might even forgive me somewhat
for being Sunflower County's leading seller
of women's dresses and women's hats and shoes.

Should I study up? Is it too late to learn the score?

TRACY LIMANTOUR
  Flowers and Smoke

A fistful of lavender lilacs
and white violets from the thick grass.
He sticks them under her nose.
"Smell them, breathe deep, Mother."
What a swell brother I have.
Mom lights up another cigarette.
"Nice, very nice, oh so nice,
now you're dirty again," she says.
Spring is blooming flowers everywhere,
but only Robby seems to care.
I love horses and yellow cats.
They never wilt in the hot sun
or shrivel up in smoky rooms.
"Don't pick any more lilacs," Mom says.
"I will if I want to," Robby says,
and bangs the door three times.

VANCE DOUGLAS
Rain Check

Arrived late with two first-game boys
at Comiskey Park in Chicago.
Bought them peanuts and hot dogs,
a program, and two pennants.
Nothing to nothing after one inning,
but the White Sox loaded the bases
in the bottom of the second frame
and I said, "Here we go, here we go."
And the boys stood up, cheered wildly,
and stamped their feet on peanut shells
and crammed hot dogs into fanatic mouths.
Then the rain came down and down
and there was a two-hour rain delay,
before the contest was canceled
amongst moans and curses and loud boos.
So we drove back to Alliance
in all the sun a ballpark could want.
Oh crap, crap, crap on old Lady Luck.
Look what she's done to my boys,
who think their dad is a foul-ball dad.
And my "Cheer up, there's another day"
is greeted with a grandstand of groans.

CRAIG BARNET
Tune Box

I'm here with my ex-wife at her house.
It has been a long week of no sunshine.
Some shriveled leaves zigzag past the window.
"I want something to believe in," she says.
"Death is the final dance of life," I say.
"What? What? What are you saying?" she says.
"Leaves always die this time of year," I say.
"They can't hang on anymore, that's all."
She picks a gray hair off her gray slacks.
"I'm not talking about the season," she says.
I make up my mind to change the subject.
"You have the tune box turned down too low," I say.
"I'm not happy with the songs lately," she says.
"No rhythms that make you want to dance?" I say.
She paces the room in her broken shoes.
Another leaf falls in the puddled yard.
"There's a tune that croons of paradise," I say.
"It's a pink islands in the sun song."
"Paradise? Don't make me laugh," she says.
I squeeze her shoulder and walk out the door.
I turn on the radio in the truck.
Life is just a rocky road of rock lyrics.
I hear Stevie Wonder, Billy Joel,
and then I wonder "What a Fool Believes."

JOSHUA KING
Bread and Apples

It was the day before Easter.
At the river, near the highway bridge,
I watched the rain turn to sleet
and the sleet turn to snow.
It was cold and I had no cap,
no gloves, and only a light coat.
I was there to feed the ducks.
Bread for ducks, a red apple for me.
I saved some food for the lame duck
who lost a foot when he got caught
in some tangled wire by the dam,
and who was found almost starved to death
by a girl who had apple cheeks
redder than Raggedy Ann's.
At last I saw him, gimping along,
coming to where I waited with bread.
"Here you go, old buddy," I said,
and gave him some big hunks.
I ate my apple down to the core
and tossed it into the river.
The ducks waddled around
on the muddy shore for awhile
and went back to their cold-water home.
I got up the slippery bank
and walked across the highway bridge,
crowded with Easter shoppers.
I bought more bread and apples
at the new market on the Square.
"Don't forget to feed the wildlife,"
I said to the checkout lady.
"Wildlife? What wildlife?" she said.
"Find some," I said. "Find some."
Then I slogged through the slushy park
to my room at the Lincoln Arms.

DREW MANNING
Harvest Dust

The carnival rays of the sun
illuminated the dust clouds
that rose behind a blue combine
harvesting forty-two acres
of good Illinois soybeans.
I stood there quietly,
the evening breeze around my head,
watching the dust thicken,
seeing emeralds and red tapestries,
seeing golden showers of rain.
Then the sun dropped behind
the last stretch of prairie,
and once again the dust
became no more than dust
in the cool and farm-dark air.

ABIGAIL TAYLOR
Senility

At the city dump we saw
a bathtub with three feet.

Frank James made me black tea.
There are no lilies in our valley.
Nothing but lies about that man.
I want violets for my hair.

At the city dump we saw
a broom with two straws.

I did too know him, I did so too.
And that's why I spoke to him.
I knew him in Keokuk, Iowa.
And that's why he spoke to me.

At the city dump we saw
a stool with one leg.

The boy who loves me has a knife.
This is a funny place to stop.
Those birds are angry at me again.
I'll run away when I have to.

At the city dump we saw
a rag doll with no face.

HAZEL JORDAN
Puberty

Sunday school
never had
a beggar's chance
once he went through
the beaded curtain
of puberty.
One morning
he woke up
to a louder tune,
reached for
a hotter flame.
Girls were
no longer dummies
to throw
mulberries
or green walnuts at.
His Bible
gathered dust
on the dresser.
He spent more time
in the bathroom,
with the door locked.
He still went
with us
to St. Peter's
now and then,
but there was
no more talk
about his wanting
to be a priest.
His moods changed
from week to week,
even, it seemed,
from day to day.
"I don't know
what's gone wrong,"
he said to me.

"My life
was all hammered out,
all set,
but things are
jumbled now
and I'm so confused."
Under his bed
I found
a cheap magazine
full of nude women
showing
all they got.
Last Tuesday
he turned sixteen.
I heard rumors
that he and Brenda,
just down the block,
were seen
in the bushes.
I prayed for him
and blew
the dust off
his Bible.

PRUDENCE ARCHER
   Thirteen

There are girl dreams I can make out of snow,
always using this house in snowfall December,
a wedding cake house with pretty me in a snow-white dress,
ready to descend the staircase and disappear in snow,
off to the snowy Episcopal church and my wedding day.

These snow-cloud dreams of marriage vows and bridal cakes
have been going on for many snowball winters,
although I'm just thirteen and my snow-hating sisters
were married not in snow but in May, June, and September.

I'm Prudence Archer and I believe in snow.

ISAIAH ROODHOUSE
Putting Off the Encyclopedia Salesman

No, the wife is not home just now.
Well, actually, she's home,
but she's back in our corn patch
picking out some ripe ones for supper.
With all the corn growing
in Sunflower County, Illinois,
you probably think it's a bit strange
we should want it in the yard too.
But the corn tassel, mister,
is my special, personal idiom.
I love to look at corn, eat corn,
and even think about corn.
What we have around here
is good corn air and good corn earth.
And you can hear corn growing:
whispering, crackling sounds.
Cornstalks, corn leaves, cornhusks,
corn silk, corn kernels—
I'll call in the wife, if you want,
but she'll side in with me.
As I said, we have four encyclopedias,
and the other books we've bought
are near to taking over the house.

KYLE TROWBRIDGE
Bird's-Eye View

Ken is not the adventuresome kind.
When I told him there was a great view
of the western half of Prairie Street
from the top of his very own pine tree
and that he sure ought to make the trip,
as it was damn well worth all the sweat,
he informed me in no uncertain words:
"Why climb up there just to look at
some more of what is right down here?"
"It's different, so different," I said.
"The tops of roofs, the spread of yards.
What you see is what a bird can see."
Then I climbed back up the tall pine
and called down the news that Amy Scott
was sunbathing with her halter off.
He frowned and I knew it was no use
to talk to one so alive yet so dead.
"Big deal," he said, and closed his eyes.

PIKE WALDROP
For the Record

The telephone poles have flowered with posters again:
WALDROP FOR SENATOR and I LIKE PIKE.

I sit here in the White Star Pharmacy these days.
Let my old cronies yammer at the Square.

She said to me, my daughter's little daughter,
"Grandfather, they named a big clock for you."

Three thought Lincoln the best, four favored Roosevelt,
but I stuck up for Herbert Clark Hoover.

I have a gold railroad watch in my vest pocket
and a democratic hole in my right shoe.

I'm against taxes—usually; war—generally;
and sin, suffering, crime, and corruption.

There are some traditional American smells here:
root beer, bacon fat, a good Tampa-made cigar.

Out at the dairy farm I have six stuffed owls
and a huge Cal Coolidge campaign poster.

The Republic is all I ever worried my head about.
Where is it now they bury the bones of circus horses?

MICHAEL FLANAGAN
Unemployed

In this tall frame house
with a turret and a weather vane,
I, Michael Flanagan,
a lumpy, round-shouldered guy
who too closely resembles
a sack of grain broken open,
sit at my rolltop desk
and draw tiny Ferris wheels
on a Trailways timetable.
Between window and bookcase
are my signed and sealed diplomas.
How does that old saying go:
"Never criticize the trapper
with the skins on the wall"?
Maybe so, but I still want a job.
There is no fun in living
second or third class.
I remember prim, blue-haired ladies
in a dumpy Wisconsin tavern
near the Soo Line tracks
drinking Potosi beer
and saying to each other,
"This is better than the Ritz"
and "It's great to slum it."
And a millhand turned to
a crane operator and said,
"What's this world coming to?"
An open book is what I want chiseled
on my marble gravestone,
and these simple words,
He never got off the bus.
Coming from a place so small
that the tallest building
was an Arco station,
I should have been prepared
to hear advice for the unemployed,
such as the mailman's
"Perhaps you can catch on
at the car wash across town."

94

I gaze at the sheepskins
tacked neatly to the wall
and slump in my chair.
I am an empty burlap bag now,
the loose grain of my body
falling on the bare floorboards,
my tired, feeble thoughts turning
to carnival lights blowing
in the big Midwestern wind,
my father coming out
of the beer tent again,
his Irish-American face
red as a brakeman's flag.

WHITEY PHILLIPS
The Red Dress

She may never be as well known
as the woman dressed in red
who set up famous John Dillinger
in front of the Biograph theater
that night in Chicago.
But she's red in her own right,
her dress as red as red can hope to be,
sitting in a wide wicker chair,
smiling once, trying to smile again,
not conscious of being pretty,
being a bit too young for that.
I snap a half dozen photos of her,
try hard to get the perfect shot
of an only daughter
who has turned four years old today.
She's a punkin, no doubt of that,
so winning even John Dillinger
might very well have bought her
a candy cane or ice cream cone,
or yahoo cocky after ditching
some hapless Hoosier cop on a dirt road,
he might have poked a silver dollar
into her little white hand.
Done now with picture taking,
we're off to the movies,
and all I can say to her is,
"Here's looking at you, kid."

GARY SHACKHAMMER
Remembering the Thirties

The clock ticks in the hall, ticks in the hall, ticks . . .

Roy's Model T Ford rusts behind the mortgaged barn.
Goldenrod grows through a hole in the runningboard.

Our daddy never did come home from the turkey shoot.
"He was last seen in East Moline," says the deputy.

They say things on the farm are all going to pot.
In the towns there is a steady growth of Hoovervilles.

Huddled by the radio, we listen to Roosevelt speak.
We nod our heads and chew stale bread-heels with
    mayonnaise.

The morning westbound freight is crammed with
    men out of work.
Karl draws a NRA blue eagle on the calendar.

"Sew and sew: the whole country's gone to stitches,"
    Ma says.
My pants are shot; Steve's coat belongs to Timothy.

Peggy's new buffalo nickel rolls down the storm drain.
Now there's nothing more that jingles in her piggybank.

Uncle Cornelius moves in with us in June.
In August we all move in with Aunt Winifred.

The clock ticks in the hall, ticks in the hall, ticks . . .

CHICK CUNNINGHAM
Horse Opera

Cowboy movie with John Wayne.
And I have popcorn and my gun.
But I'm still in a jail of grief.
Some ornery dude rustled my bike.

Mary Lou is a pretty keen sis.
She pats me gently on the knee.
Squaws know when a kid is down.
John's horse just got shot.

It was plenty tough out west.
You had to be right on your toes.
John sure drinks a lot of beer.
Now how can I ride to school?

My pa gets madder than John does.
He may not listen to the truth.
Indians being nasty to whites.
Take that, and that, bad guys.

STELLA LYNCH
The Opposite Sex

You bet he was there last Saturday night,
him with all that bleached blond hair,
with his thunder and lightning shirt,
with his merry-go-round pants,
with his dude-ranch cowboy boots.
He was liquored up like a payday coal miner.
He made no effort to dance with any of us.
He was looking all over for you,
asking everybody where you was at.
"Say, where's May, where's May?" he says,
popping his gum, grinning like a fool.
If you ask me, he's a real creep.
I'd like to see him mess around after me.
I got an old man and two brothers
which are all about half crazy.
They'd pour gasoline on top of him
and melt that tail of his down to the ground.
It's guys like him what take all the fun
out of all these country-western dances.
There's always at least one of his type,
always someone with a Texas-size mouth
and some refried beans for brains.
If I was you, I'd stay the hell away
from the Amoco station, the Dew Drop Inn,
from the Sunset Bowling Lanes,
from the corner of Sixth and Park,
and the roller rink too, if I could.
But, hey, pay no mind to me, May.
There's some of you peculiar folks
who just can't wait to take on trouble.

DAVID MOSS
Corn and Beans

You won't believe it, Uncle Max.
The corn is already scarecrow high
and those beans are swelling up,
proud as new granddaddies.

What we have here, my boy,
is some good old-fashioned
ag-ri-cul-ture.

Corn wants to fly away, Uncle Max,
and beans want to spread their fire.

Son, the sun is surely gospel.

ROXANNE RUSSELL
  Getting Caught

My dad says he's a Populist.
He says what that means is that
he's a person who doesn't like
all the changes that have been going on
in this wacky world,
that everyone has gone blind,
but knows, too, it's too late
to do much about fixing things,
but, hey, why not raise a lot of hell,
scream, yell, throw a fit anyhow.

He sure did that this afternoon,
sneaking down the stairs snaky like
in his slippers and silk bathrobe
and catching Dee Dee Watson and I,
naked as catfish,
wrestling and fooling around
on the recreation room rug.
There was no car in the driveway.
I thought Dad was at work.
Dee Dee has a great body. I love her.

EDGAR WILSON
Carousel

We're at the Sunflower County Fair.
I stand in noon's dusty heat.
Polly rides a spotted pony.
That's sure a catchy calliope tune.
The midway people press about me.
Sweat smells and perfume smells.
The odor of cooking grease.
There, that is my daughter.
I want to say it out loud.
Little kewpie doll sweetheart.
Round goes the merry-go-round.
Dizzy. I'm getting dizzy.
It must be the humidity.
Or I'm up too close.
There's laughter on the summer wind.
There's not a cloud in the sky.
Is everybody happy?
I look around and smile.
Just good Midwestern folks here.
Grand Wood's plain women.
Farmers without pitchforks.
A flock of 4-H girls.
Dentists on their day off.
Boy in bib overalls cracks peanuts.
Pink cotton candy kisses my ear.
Hot dogs and hamburgers.
Ice cream bars and ice-cold lemonade.
This is Polly's third ride.
Quite enough, I'd say.
The music stops.
The ponies stop.
But she won't get down.
Holds the reins tightly.
You got to know how to handle kids.
Use a little tenderness.
"Be Daddy's good girl."
But she screams.
"Quit that. Quit that at once."
Some nincompoop laughs his head off.
It's that bowlegged bronchobuster.

The bastard.
All right, I'll have to be firm.
I put on my mad face.
Of course the rubes are staring.
That's hicks for you.
Wonderful.
Now she's soiled her pants.
"Get down, do you hear me?"
I grab her arm and pull.
Her eyes blaze into small fires.
"I won't, I won't, I won't," she says.
Just like her mother.
Damn Dutch stubborn.
No, it can never be.
I can't love this brat.
Help!

MICHELLE TREMBLAY
Yellow

Not fearful,
not afraid to speak out,
and not Chinese,
no, but yellow skin
the color of old newsprint,
or an aged sunflower
if you happen to catch him
leaning up against
a light pole or picket fence
some morning in late September.
Yellow hat, too,
and often a mustard shirt
or butter-colored pants.
We call him "Yellow,"
or "The Yellow Man."
He knows it,
he's heard it many times,
yes, and he knows it's not because
he's scared of fights,
or bullies, or anything.
Oh, yellow, yellow,
he's always looking like
a yellow teddy bear,
the kind you found
in your childhood attic
on those long winter Sundays.
Look, here he is now,
coming at us,
breaking in a pair
of yellow-bean shoes.

REV. FELIX DIETRICH
Gospel

I'm thinking about those
boot prints up and down
the kitchen floor,
a foiled bank heist
over in DeKalb County,
and the sermon I can't write
for Thanksgiving week.
Now what is "humble"?
And what is "grateful"?
I know what chickens are:
big thundering trouble,
at least when your son
goes off and steals one.
"You don't know turkeys,"
I tell him, kind of mad.
What I told the sheriff was,
"You got lawman's tracks
from your muddy boots
right up to my freezer,
I don't hold with stealing,
and as far as I'm concerned
Bob's a good boy."
My sermon on Sunday
is going to be one I stole
off this Okie preacher
during the Dust Bowl years.
It's here in the files
along with my clippings
of the Younger brothers.

VICKI ST. CLAIR
Home from the River

The air is green.
We walk home barefoot.
Our bodies are heavy with heat
and my nose is sunburned.
The tops of houses and trees
are scribbles on a child's scratch pad.
The river we just left
moves south in moist darkness.
A firefly lights its flare.
There is no wind.

TRAVIS JOHNSTON
North

Haze hangs heavy in the slow September air.
A freight train crawls through parched cornfields
and past backyards strung with shirts and jeans.
A troop of sunflowers slumps across the fence.
The sour-mash sky around the collapsed silo
is the color of George Dickel's best whiskey.
Jake Cotton's barn says CHEW MAIL POUCH TOBACCO.
The bald brakeman leans from his yellow caboose
and, smiling, waves to me, and I wave to him.
Down in Tennessee I had many friendly fathers.
But I'm in Illinois now, on northern soil,
lonesome in the long shadow of Abe Lincoln's name.

RANDY WHITE
From a Big Chief Tablet Found Under
a Bench at the Courthouse Square

Katy will only kiss me now
when we crouch among
the tall cornstalks
off Potawatomi Road.

I think she thinks she's
Pocahontas,
hiding from the gunshot eyes
that would scorch her flesh.

Last night in a hugging fog
an Illinois state trooper
roared up the blacktop
like a wild beast on fire.

Katy bit her sore lip,
and it bled
and bled
on mine.

BREW AMES
Boogers

So I loaned him
four Superman comic books
and asked for them back
three days later,
but he said he wasn't done
with them, and I said
I wasn't done
with them either and wanted
to keep them for good
and always, and
two Tuesdays after that I
went up to his house
and said to him,
"Well, where are my Superman
comic books?" and he
said nothing and
just handed them over and
closed the door, but it
didn't make me
happy to get them back and
it was no wonder,
seeing what he
had done to them, because there
were these pages stuck
together with
boogers, so I called him out
of his house and said,
"Look, Rusty, you
asshole, you can keep these old
Superman comic
books, for they're no
good to me now and I don't
want them anymore,
and I don't want
us to be friends, either, so
goodbye to you and
your booger face."

109

SHERRY LARKIN
Two on the Farm

He blew me a kiss
when I brought in the mail,
but I didn't see him.
Later, I waved to him
when he took out the garbage,
but he didn't see me.
Now, heavy fog has moved in
to isolate the farm,
and we are more unseeing than ever.
So that's why
I must tell you this:
Please don't drive
too far out of your way
to see us this time,
for we may be as blind to you
as we are to each other.
And what a sad weekend
that would be.

BRIDGET RICE
Motorcycle Accident

My brother drank milk and light beer,
chewed only sugarless gum,
would eat nothing fried or fatty,
jogged, worked out at a fitness center,
got to bed before ten o'clock,
took cold morning showers.
I did none of these things and laughed at him.
He said I'd be sorry someday,
and he was right about that,
but not sorry for what he said
I'd be sorry about,
about not watching my health.

Last Saturday we buried my brother
in Blackberry Hill Cemetery.
Everyone cried. He was beautiful.
He could stand on his head,
tear telephone books with his teeth,
hold his breath under water the longest time.
I scattered sunflower seeds on his grave,
stayed drunk for several days.
My mother said to me, "Why, why?"
My father said to me, "Why, why, why?"
How the hell do I know why.
Tell me, does like make any sense?

111

LILLIAN EDWARDS
In Fear of Old Age

I have been here too long.
I am tired of stumbling about
my cold limestone farmhouse.
Through the afternoon fog
the amber headlight
of a slow westbound freight
freezes me by the tracks.
March fields are streaked with snow.
The farmhouse is a landmark.
Everyone knows where I live.
I am scared to death
I will just creep on forever.

The train's dull-eyed headlight
is a bug-encrusted bulb
found in old-fashioned rooms.

Too long, way too long.

Wet snow on broken ground.
My body is part farm, part house,
and both are crumbling.

Too long, way too long.

Scream of diesel horn.
Iron wheels pound in my head.
My eyes are cold limestone.

Too long, way too long.

HOWARD DRUMGOOLE
Hotel Tall Corn

You know, I sorta, kinda like it.

It's not very tall at all,
and the only corn about the old place
is dispensed by the night desk clerk,
who's been around since Alf Landon
stopped being presidential timber.

The beds are soft, the plumbing works.

If you miss the last bus out of town,
that's where you go to get some sleep.

One cold, gloomy December evening
I slogged through half-frozen slush
to attend a wedding reception,
held in the swankiest suite they had.
The next morning the groom was found
hanging by his farmer's red neck
in a round barn west of Rochelle.

Woody Herman's band played there once,
a real "Woodchopper's Ball."

I hope it stays alive a little while.

It's the kind of rube hotel
Sherwood Anderson would hole up in
to write about the beauty of horses,
the faded dreams of small-town girls,
and the lives of lovesick millhands.

You know, I sorta, kinda like it.

CLIFF PECOTA
Mud, Oil, and Jello

"I've wrestled women in mud
and in oil, but tonight
at the Club Safari
it will be in jello,"
she said, and set down
my hotcakes, sausage, and eggs.
She was made for combat,
a husky, spirited girl
who liked to show off
her body to the boys.
I had recently worked
a job with her father,
putting in more toilets
at the country club.
"Where are you working now?"
she said, her elbows
on the counter, her eyes
watching me eat breakfast.
"The Ford agency,"
I said, "selling cars,
or trying to, anyway."
In the third grade we sat
next to each other
at Seventh Street School.
I still remember the day
we made some big cutout
Thanksgiving turkeys
out of thick brown paper
and the teacher, Miss Luby,
stuck them on the windows.
One afternoon I stopped by
her house after school.
Her stepmother gave us
store-bought cookies and milk,
then shooed us out to play
on the backyard jungle gym.
In high school she was
terrific at softball
and set records in track.
"Jello, huh? Jello?"

I said, mopping syrup
with the last scrap of hotcake.
"I think I'll drop by
at the Club Safari.
I've never seen you do it
in jello, not jello."
"Yeah, it was mud at first,
then oil for a few years,
but it's mostly jello now,"
she said, flexing a bicep.
"Well, I'll be damned, jello,"
I said. "What next, eh?"
She poured me more coffee.
"If it's jello they want,
I'll wrestle in jello,"
she said, and giggled.
I could tell she was getting
excited about her match.
She breathed heavily and her
breasts moved up and down.
"Mud was fun, but I think
I liked you best in oil,"
I said, and left with a wink,
a salute, and a smile.

JEREMY FORQUER
The Smell of Lilacs

I took the shortcut across the park.
The dew soaked my new suede shoes.
Through the green dusk I saw your yard light.
I could smell lilacs everywhere.
Someone was playing a piano.
That's my Stephanie Jane, I thought.
I knocked on the kitchen door.
The house was full of strangers.
They all said they didn't know you.
I walked back to the hotel.
A low branch scraped my forehead.
Sudden tears welled up in my eyes.
I should have written, should have phoned.
Three years of my life withered on the grass.
A crippled dog nipped at my heels.
I hate the small of lilacs.

ARDIS NEWKIRK
At the Charity Ball

For something to say, he said:
"I just love greenhouses with their steamy heat
and all those small plants growing tall there.
And I love woodchucks and gymnastics
and crickets and oatmeal cookies.
I can tell chicory from prairie clover.
Down by the tracks where Stacy Engle lives
there's gobs of it right this minute.
I know the names of all the townships
they have here in Sunflower County,
all the trees, and all the birds that fly around.
Do you like player pianos? I do.
The Donovans next door have one, you know,
and they start it up every now and again
and Mrs. Donovan makes loads of lemonade
and we shoo the flies away and laugh a lot.
They also still have their old
1928 RCA Radiola
and a chair George Ade once sat on.
I can tell swamp frogs from tree frogs.
Sure, I think Black Hawk got a bum deal.
I also think it's a terrible scandal
they have discontinued Old Settlers Day."

For something to say, I said:
"Harrison Stanley Hudepohl, shut up.
You know I don't like to talk when I'm dancing!"

GARTH LIGHT
Muscles

I'm lifting weights in a sweaty barn.

Gail is a shy, star-kissed windmill
turning gently on a bed of air,
her long legs the color of goldenrod
under the strong and mating sun.

I'm grunting. I'm gasping. I'm groaning.

I'm Garth, her bulging lover,
a silo standing between horse and house,
steely-eyed, mute, but lovable,
a bruiser with massive thighs.

I'm building muscles I'll never use.

RICHARD GARLAND
Railroad Strike

The radio says
the trains aren't running
for another day.

When the railroaders
go out on strike
in the dead of winter,
the frozen ground
of northern Illinois
loses its iron music.
Folks who live near the tracks
get a little jumpy.
Something familiar
has been switched off.
There is nothing now
to hold together
the body's old rhythms.

A thin, stooped woman,
wrapped in a heavy muffler
and blowing white ghosts
of zero-degree breath,
slams the back door,
flips away a cigarette,
and tips over a basket
of two dozen or so green bottles
into an empty oil drum.
The noise is like a bomb.
Across the way shades fly up.
A man slips on the ice.
Thirteen dogs bark wildly.

A blizzard wind
rattles the windows
of the abandoned caboose.

CHARLOTTE NORTHCOTT
  Insomnia

The moonlight on this spring night is simply dazzling.
One thousand brides are dancing in white wedding gowns.

Sixty-four coal cars clanked over the rail joints,
clickety-clacked right into Alliance, Illinois.

The latest wedding pictures fill the weekly *Gazette.*
I read all the names and hate all the happy faces.

Every last coal car was piled high with lumps of coal,
which sparkled there in the frosty March moonshine.

But where is *my* lover, *my* dreamer of marriage feasts?
Is he asleep, a moonbeam kissing his collarbone?

Oh you seekers of true beauty, where were you tonight
when a whole trainload of diamonds danced through town?

120

JUNIOR IVES
Barn Burner

After Petersen's barn burned
on that warm Indian summer night,
we all sat around the kitchen table
and drank from a full-moon of apple cider,
saying "You did it, you did it,
you set fire to Seth Petersen's barn,"
pointing accusing fingers at one another
and laughing to beat the devil.
Oh, I carried on with the best of them,
with Ma and Cousin Annabelle,
with Leroy and dumb Carl and Virgil,
with Uncle Roger and Aunt Alice.
And they never suspected me,
never knew why I was crazy for cold cider,
my throat parched the way it was
from the red excitement of flames,
from running across dry corn-stubble,
my pockets bulging with matches.

LOGAN STUART
   The Union Soldier

Under a corn-green moon
on this first warm night in May,
you, our Union soldier,
throw away your rifle,
light up a brierroot pipe,
and scratch your balls.

Damnit, man, that's no way to do.
Not with the last show just let out
at the Paradise theater,
and me all set to walk Elsie Kraft,
the new Alliance librarian,
back home down Lincoln Street.

And I suppose you know by now
that Joel Bothwell's little sister
is grabbing herself
a big whopping eyeful,
and the girls from the dime store
are giggling up a storm.

And see, too, Judge Otto Taylor,
over by the popcorn machine,
jabbing hysterically
with his hickory cane
and shouting, "whippersnapper,"
"hooligan," "degenerate."

Sure, I know, I know,
there's a Union soldier like you
standing tall on every courthouse lawn
in the good old Middle West.
And you're dead right,
we do take you boys for granted.

But next time you get the itch
to be noticed, my young friend,
why not sing "Lorena," say.
Oh hell, that's a Rebel song.
Well, maybe you can whistle a tune
softly through your teeth.

It seems to me we'd all kind of go
for a bit of that stuff
around these here parts,
this fractured-skull town
being so slugged with silence
and never much musical.

BARBARA HAWKINS
 Anteaters

Listen,
the real reason
they don't have
anteaters
in Animal Crackers
is because
anteaters
would make
all the other
animals
laugh themselves
to pieces,
and when
you opened the box
there would be
just crumbs.

PEGGY DANIELS
Moonlight Yodel

"In the pale moonlight" is a cliché,
so I won't use it in my down-home poem
about our stroll last night across your farm,
a stroll that took us to corncribs,
roll of barbed wire, rusted water pump,
cedar trees, stacked elm logs, orchard grass,
small hill of shelled corn, tumbleweed, mailbox.
I won't use "stroll" either, by golly,
because that's a word a bit too cute
for an outback Illinois word slinger.
And, come to think about it, my man,
walking-in-the-moonlight poems are old hat.
Instead, I'll write about how you woke up
the Beauchamp family, a dozen dogs,
sixteen cats, and who knows how many birds,
when you proved to me you could yodel.
"I'm from Yellow Medicine County," you said,
as if that explained the whole thing.

SHIRLEY JELLICOE
Neighbor

So sad. Too bad
she had to die
of flu. I thought
she was all right.
She'll be missed at
the dry goods store
and the beauty
parlor. Good grief,
I did not know
her heat had been
turned off and she
was sick in bed,
too proud no doubt
to phone for help.
Not that she'd cry
out to her mean
old brother and
his sour wife on
that frozen farm
they have up north
near the state line.
But, look, she could
have thought of me.
That hurts. I thought
I was the best
old friend she had.
Too bad. So sad.

MAURY CHASE
Famous

One time while waiting for a haircut,
I read a story in some magazine
about how this famous American painter,
Thomas Hart Benton, no less,
chewed Days Work tobacco,
and having taken up watercolors
and aiming to get at oils, too,
wondered if that would help me somewhat
in my life's one big ambition.

Well, I bought a supply of the stuff
and got right down to work,
doing a picture of a pickle crock,
slaving there under the tulip tree,
braving the insects and the summer heat,
and then it was finished
and it was very, very good,
so I kept on chewing and spitting
and won second prize at the Art Fair.

To be famous you got to know how.

SONNY BAXTER
Spider Webs

I hunker on the porch
and stare at spider webs.
They tell me Father hated Jews
and Jews hated Father.
Now what is that to me?
I run my middle finger
over the bottom step
where the wood's gone mush.
Shoes, you clomp and clomp.
Shoes, you keep on coming,
going nowhere,
returning from nothing.
A crimson maple leaf
falls on my outstretched hand.
I tear it with my teeth,
then chomp it,
chew it to bits.
It was too beautiful.
It put a hurt high in my heart.
Grandpa crosses the grass,
the *Chicago Tribune* at his hip.
The old boy has chicken legs
and his nose is hard to blow.
The sunlight hangs dusty.
I can smell cat shit
and a cheap cigar.
There's nonsense in the kitchen.
Can't Grandma laugh her age?
Spider webs are evil.
They trap the unwary,
the too adventurous.
Spider webs are wrapped around
Alliance, around Illinois,
around the whole U.S. of A.
I stretch flat on my back
and listen to Baptist bells
and the wham-bam
of slammed doors.

Mother always went to church
in her gaudiest glad rags.
Father mowed the lawn
or stuck those watery eyes
in the bowels of his Chrysler.
No, Sunday's nothing special.
I aim to keep it so.

KENNETH SANDSTROM
Crazy in California

Now, she writes a letter from
a hard-shell state mental home,
says, "I don't know where I am,
someone ran off with my old face,
the trees aren't friendly here,
and the Duke of Oil
wants to have sex with me."

Now, California is no place
for a Sunflower County girl
to take her teenage troubles to
and wind up behind blank walls,
not a wild-strawberry girl,
a don't-stop-the-merry-go-round girl,
a girl looking for kinky kicks.

Now, with nothing new to say,
I drop her a few lines
and remind her of the time
back in sky-high high school
when we ate cold pork chops
on her grandmother's antique bed
and said, "Ain't life grand?"

DUKE NICHOLS
Domestic

She had shampooed her red hair
and pulled down a wool cap to her ears.
I sat at the bare kitchen table
in my bathrobe and paint-stained slippers.
She went up to the Hotpoint stove
to warm up some chicken soup.
Her tiny head looked very much like
a windscreen on a microphone.
"What's wrong with driving a truck?" I said,
and bit into a kosher pickle.
She turned and gave me a sour look.
"We've been over that before," she said.
"You're not giving up your job
with Farm and Fleet, no sir, no way,
to go haul-assing all over hell
in a goddamn trailer truck."
The soup boiled and we ate it.
"I don't want to argue," I said.
"You have your throbbing toothache
and I have this hangover."
"Don't bring it up again if you
don't want to argue," she said.
"Yes, a windscreen on a microphone.
That's what your head looks like," I said.
"What's that?" she said, slurping soup.
"I think I'll lie down somewhere.
I feel rotten, real punk," I said.
"You ought to lie down somewhere," she said,
and stared at the ironing board.

TOM RANDALL
Under a Gigantic Sky

There's a milkweed butterfly
kissing Barbara Allen's knee.

Yep, I'm going to fall in love again.

We live near a burned-out roller rink,
the Chicago and North Western tracks,
and a field of tornado-toppled corn.

Barbara Allen sleeps in the shade
on the warm, pine-scented grass.

Oh, man, it hurts me so good.

We have been here forever in this place,
drifting under a gigantic sky,
lost on the golden prairies of America.

A breeze lifts Barbara Allen's skirt
above her hips, above her head.

Wow!

The whole damned Middle West
is looking
up.

VERNON YATES
  Talking About the Erstwhile Paperboy
  to the Editor of the *Alliance Gazette*

Mister, he was an awkward, gangly son of a gun
and, if it's truth you're asking for,
just a little bit on the homely side too.

He whipped around here on a battered blue bicycle,
making faces, doing tricks on the handlebar.
What a cutup that kid was, a genuine show-off.

He was kind of sweet on my Penelope for awhile,
until the Turner twins, Ted and Tod, put him straight.
They told him to go peddle his papers, and we all laughed.

The boy was sure reliable, I'll say that for him.
No one on Prairie Street ever had to beg the headlines.
It's a real shame he's dead, and so young.

He was with a patrol behind the enemy lines, it seems.
They got ambushed by the gooks and chopped to pieces.
That's all I know, that's all I heard.

Well, I'll always see him there in the news agency,
rolling up those Chicago dailies and shouting,
"You'll never see me in any Vietnam!"

URSULA ZOLLINGER
Last House on Union Street

The mother, who has read all the Latin poets,
sitting in a wicker chair, mending old socks,
waiting for a cooling breeze, skirts hiked up.

She was paying no attention to—

The two children, who have read all the Oz books,
sitting on a bench, trying their best
to eat a whole box of chocolate-covered cherries.

They were paying no attention to—

The father, who has read all of Ring Lardner,
sitting on the porch steps, smoking thin cigars,
lighting kitchen matches with his thumbnail.

He was paying no attention to—

The college boy, who has read all of Marx,
sitting in the hammock, dreaming up a scheme
to sell *Praying Hands*, the framed *Blond Jesus*.

GLENN TWITCHELL
Rose Petals

Look, I can't help it any if Lola Jean
chews on those pale pink rose petals
when she walks to the Catholic church
or downtown to buy a spool of thread.
And I can't worry no more that son Jack
may swallow his chaw of bubble gum
while playing tag with the Tyson kids.
Aunt Rhoda said it right, all right:
'This family of yours is never, ever
without something in their mouths,
something dangling, something dancing,
kitchen matches, ice cream sticks,
a wad of paper, a blade of grass,
anything to bite on, anything to suck."
That's right, Auntie, my mouth is dry,
my teeth itch, my lips are lonesome.
Nails, pencils, toothpicks, car keys,
they are all here when I need them.
"Do we have any jujubes left?"
says my wife, rummaging a candy sack.

PERRY MEEK
Wife Killer

Now please pay attention, children.
The cedar chest
that Daddy has put down in the cellar
is not to be played with,
not to be used in hide-and-seek
or in any of your other games.
I hope this is clear, children,
for I don't want to have to get mad
and use my leather belt on you again.
Just pretend there's a blue monster
sleeping in that chest
who loves to eat little boys and girls.
Let's make this our new game, shall we?
And I'll play with you.
I'll be scared of the monster too.
And no more nonsense, children,
about Mother having fun with us,
keeping quiet, waiting to be found.
Damn it, I told you a thousand times
that she's not here anymore.
She's away, visiting in Vincennes.
That's where Grandma lives.
Remember?
Again, keep out of that cellar.
Do you understand me, John?
Do you, Miss Prudence?
Well, say something.
Answer me!
Oh my, oh my, oh my.
Daddy's losing patience, children.

DENISE WATKINS
Some Come Running

When she comes in from school,
I kiss her cold, bright cheek,
she having walked the six blocks home
in February's near-zero weather,
or probably not walked at all but ran
and maybe ran almost all the way,
but did not run because it was cold and February
but ran the way a child will run
when she's happy about school or home or both
and wants to shorten the time between the two,
happy to be at either place
and wanting you to know it's true.

And so she is standing here
just a little out of breath,
warming now in the oven-warm kitchen,
and I pull off her boots for her
and help her with her coat,
and then get out the silver Christmas comb
to comb the fierce tangles from her hair.

We are deep in the middle
of a long, quiet afternoon.
There is nothing planned or scheduled,
nothing special for us to do.

But that's all right, that's good too.

JUBAL MONTGOMERY
Oddball

It's me I'm talking about,
Jubal, this town's number one oddball,
Henry Miller's *Tropic of Cancer*
in my sweaty left hand,
a twist of marijuana between my lips,
ambling along the deserted back roads,
taking notes on the ways of cows,
the mysteries of crows and corn,
spitting into the country wind
and getting my face wet.
Yes, that's me, that's me,
part hipster, part hayseed,
a combination I've learned to live with,
the white cat of innocence
crouched before the dark door of experience.
Hey there, is that a cow or a bull?
No matter now, it's coming too close
and it doesn't look friendly.
I toss away my crazy smoke,
squeeze Henry Miller,
and beat it back down the road.
When I reach my attic room,
I'll play a new Eric Dolphy album,
stuff my corncob with Union Leader,
drink a tall glass of Ma's rhubarb wine.

WALLY DODGE
The Hat

He sure had a mess of fishhooks on that hat.
Of course he didn't have it on his head,
because he was still working, working hard,
still on duty at Fred's gasoline station.
No, that hat of his was there on a telephone book,
right under the rack of highway maps.
Yes, I picked it up and looked at it, yes,
but not to look over the fishhooks.
It was the hat itself I was curious about,
having never seen a yellow hat with a green brim
and wanting to see what the label would tell me.
Who stole the hat is something I couldn't say.
I don't fish myself, and the hat didn't fit.
So I spent the rest of the day looking at tires
and watching a Jaguar get a grease job.
Say, is there anything special about that hat?
Maybe those fishhooks were made out of silver.
Or maybe the hat was imported from Peru.
I know it's no big joke to you, you being his wife
and having to live with an unhappy hatless man,
but I can't cry about it now, can I?

MONICA ROBERTS
Private Dancer

This old man said
through the loud rock
music and stale
cigarette smoke
that it was his
birthday and he
had spent two months
saving up for
just one private
dance with me and
I said I hoped
it would be worth
twenty dollars
to him and he
said he hoped so
too and I climbed
on his lap and
straddled him and
bounced up and down
and gave my thighs
a real workout
as I rubbed my
groin against his
and wondered if
his thin legs could
take much more of
my muscled weight
and I stood up
on a chair and
wiggled and rubbed
my bare bottom
on his bald head
and told him this
might grow back some
hair and I could
feel his smile through
my butt cheeks and
I gently pushed
his face into
my bosom and

beat my titties
against his lips
back and forth and
I pulled his shirt
out of his pants
and raised it and
nibbled his right
nipple and then
I was all done
and he thanked me
and kissed me on
my sweaty neck
and later on
that evening I
let him have one
of my G-strings
because look here
I know these guys
and what they like
to hold on to.

AUGUST CRABTREE
Simple Words

Plowed, seeded, cultivated, reaped:
I knew her all her life and most of mine,
her life being here on the farm, she being my wife.

She was simple, even simple minded,
so I will use simple words to simply say:
Judy was good enough to marry, good enough to bury.

DR. MALCOLM LINDSAY
Catfish and Watermelon

All day we stared at the river,
in a boat blessed with fish luck
and this woman's enormous breasts.
Now, in a tiny clapboard house
hidden by willows and trumpet vines,
mammoth Millie fries channel cat.
"How do you like it?" she asks me.
"My new scarlet nightgown, I mean."
"You're a sternwheeler caught fire,"
I tell her, "a real conflagration."
She laughs and the floorboards creak.
Wonderful!—300 pounds of female
shaking up a sudden summer storm.
When she quits it's time to eat.
Later, after the fish are just bones,
I knife open a ripe watermelon,
broad striped and thumping good.
Millie picks out a whopping piece
and goes to work with gold teeth.
The juice runs off her double chin
and trickles between hills of flesh.
She kisses me on my sunburned neck
and then bites a black seed away
that was sticking to my right ear.
She smells of islands in the sun
and old boats soaked in morning mist.
No, it's not half bad at all
to be in love with mammoth Millie,
a river gal twice my size.

RUDY GERSTENBERG
Memo to the Erie Lackawanna

This is awkward for me to say,
but I feel I must inform you
that your shabby boxcar 68401
passed through Alliance, Illinois,
just a little past noon today.
It looked like an Old West saloon after a brawl
or the battered left field fence at the ballpark.
What was particularly embarrassing
was that it was coupled between
a classy Santa Fe refrigerator car
and a shiny Illinois Central coal car.

If there was ever a boxcar
with its pants down, so to speak,
your old 68401 was it, for sure.
Both doors were slung open wide
and some clown had written the usual "clean me"
and, of course, "Kilroy was here"
in the plains of interstate dust.
Now, I want you to know, too,
I'm in love with the Erie Lackawanna.
But beat-up 68401 sure left me blue
and I ended up feeling railroaded all day.

MARSHALL COOPER
Weeping

The last time I saw Donna's mother,
she was standing in the doorway
in bare feet and tight-fitting robe,
her hair screwed up in clay-brown rags,
a wart of quince jam on her chin,
Donna's little sister at her side.
We had said goodbye a dozen times
and Donna had kissed her and kissed her.
"Alliance is so far from here,"
Donna's mother said, and blew her nose.
"Call you on Sunday," Donna said.
"We will write you often," I said.
"No you won't," Donna's mother said.
"You won't write and you won't call, either."
"Bye, Donna," her little sister said.
The last time I saw Donna's mother
she was standing in the doorway,
weeping like a rain of willow leaves.

LUCY BETH YOUNGQUIST
Thanksgiving

After the turkey, oyster dressing,
cranberries, creamed onions, yams,
nuts, fruit, pumpkin pie, and coffee,
Father takes off his Sunday shoes
and stretches out on the davenport,
giving us strict instructions for
no singing, no dancing, no loud laughing.
He quickly drops off to deep sleep,
the unread society page tented
over his fat and snoring face.

The stuffed common barn owl
gathers dust in the attic now.
It finally made Father nervous
after all those years of saying,
"But I love him, he's good company."
And like this puffy-cheeked bird,
the relatives that have come here today
for our big Thanksgiving reunion
are sent to the limbo of "who cares."
Father likes to eat and be alone.

EMMETT BEASLEY
Man Talking to Himself

Brown cigars beat green cigars.

You are a fool out of Faulkner.
A farmer finding the general store closed.

Another game? Sure thing. Cut the cards.

No more baseball on the radio.
Nothing to eat but instant grits.

Too lazy to put up storm windows.

"She was an old and furious child."
I read that somewhere.

The piano smells like a coffin.

Forget the dirty dishes, the soiled shirts.
When the fog lifts, we'll go for a spin.

Gone. The wife is gone and gone for good.

Man, easy there on the beer.
Just three cans left.

Let's hear it now for bachelorhood!

JOHNNY WILCOX
In the Barbershop

He spits tobacco juice
on the baseball news.

I stick chewed bubble gum
in the comic books.

He wears a greasy hat
and pants with no belt.

I wear a snake-head ring
and socks that don't match.

He comes hot from corncribs
cussing out bankers.

I come damp from poolrooms
talking down hustlers.

He was a circus bum
who wrestled a bear.

I was a shoeshine boy
who married a whore.

He did two years in jail
and clobbered a cop.

I went to reform school
and flattened a priest.

They know us in this town.
We kick up the dust.

ANGEL LOOK
Chicken Milk

I didn't notice
him doing it. Not
until he giggled
at my face. Then I
saw what wiggled him
funny in his chair.
John was being a
very naughty boy.
He was dropping these
pieces of chicken
into my milk. I
knocked on his messy
head with my messy
spoon. "Anybody
home in there?" I said.
John acts crazy, you
know. The way little
kids do when they want
to. He was crying
now. Mom said, "Angel,
what did you hit him
for?" I explained what
for. Mom said, "Angel,
drink up every drop
of that glass of milk
and go straight up to
your room." I told her,
"I'm not going to
drink this chicken milk
and nobody's mad
enough to make me."

TRUDY MONROE
Saturday Afternoon on Elm Street

In the green-shuttered Victorian house
the birthday party boys and girls
are playing pin-the-tail-on-the-donkey.

But the real jackass on Elm Street
is the vacuum cleaner salesman next door
who has locked his keys inside the Plymouth,
the headlights burning, the radio on,
the slain deer still tied to the hood.

The salesman's face is three shades of blue.
He walks around and around the car,
turning his shapeless hat in his hands.

The donkey is full of laughing pins.

GROVER ELY
Ancestral Home

Rebecca Ann, her head wrapped in a polka-dot scarf,
leans over the balcony and shakes out a patchwork quilt.

Down in the yard the sundial has died of too much shade.
But the white oak is a landmark, the town's pride.

All four chimneys are unsafe and haven't smoked in years.
Stepping-stones to the grape arbor are thick with moss.

I sit in the summerhouse, sip a glass of good port,
write in my journal, read the stories of Mark Twain.

Behind me, a creaky wooden gate shuts with a ghostly click.
Two or three red-orange blossoms drop off the trumpet vine.

Later on we will drink green tea and talk about the past.
On the piecrust table is a Bible with a golden key.

The ancestors who built this monumental brick home
still stare, thin lips pursed, from their oval frames.

We, the living Elys, are softer, poorer, sadder, but
we try to stay on another year, bear another Ely child.

DEXTER CADY
Calves

It was
in the
forties,
before
the girls
wore jeans
to high
school. You
couldn't
tell if
their rear
ends were
something
special
or not,
and if
they lacked
a good
pair of
breasts, you'd
look at
their calves
and pick
out a
shapely
pair and
follow
them up
and down
Main Street.
Say, it
could be
quite a
large treat,
let me
tell you.

SARAH MULLEN
Visiting Writer

"I've known you all my life," he said.
He put his hand over my hand.
His pipe, my cigarettes.
We drank nothing but Black Russians.
Bits of Kerouac, Steinbeck.
No dancing, no jukebox music.
Friends said goodbye. We waved them off.
The weather was not mentioned.
Stories about offbeat jobs way out west.
Jokes and quips about oddballs way out west.
Movies, sports never came up.
Others left the bar. We stayed on.
We danced to the jazz of our words.
On the Road. The Wayward Bus.
We drank nothing but Black Russians.
His pipe, my cigarettes.
I put my hand over his hand.
"But we've just met, David," I said.

JOE SPRAGUE
Fourteen Stones

Late summer hollyhocks grow on both sides
of an ornate iron fence
that separates Blackberry Hill Cemetery
from a row of rural mailboxes.

The names on the boxes
have been carefully lettered.
There must be no mistakes made here.
Everyone wants what is coming to him.

Whipping up the yellow dust
on my way home for a bean sandwich,
I stop my Dun-Rite Dry Cleaning truck
to reach for two magazines and a gas bill.

In the crowded graveyard,
where the bones of four generations lie,
there are fourteen Spragues
carved on fourteen stones.

I'm no longer worried about bad news
concealed in flowered envelopes,
for my kinfold are all gone now
and my own fate waits across the fence.

HERBERT TOMPKINS
The Crippled Poet's Dream

I was trying hard to write this long Civil War poem,
moving closer to the Battle of Wilson's Creek.

She was tired of her lime-green lollipop,
dropping it in a scramble of honeysuckle vine.

I was busy, wrapped in thought, deep in hot Missouri,
reviling all the wrong maps and regiments.

She was finished with her picture of the old house,
saying it was very sad we had to move away.

I was confused, blinded in a smoky cornfield,
losing my weapon, tearing my Yankee shirt.

She was digging a doll's grave for Hannah Minerva,
repeating that strange and musical name.

I was sure we were all dead now, lost in time's fable,
dreaming of leafy rivers under our sycamore tree.

CLEO BOONE
Golden Wedding Anniversary

Old now, we remember rivers,
prairie waters nudging the shores
of our picnic and playground sand.

We remember beer and bratwurst,
wildflowers, the rowboat that leaked,
oranges eaten under willows.

We remember cool blue shadows,
an occasional firecracker,
the endless games of kick-the-can.

We remember a song or two—
"Juanita," "Breautiful Dreamer,"
the banjo I found in a ditch.

We also remember bodies:
tan thighs, pale buttocks, a wet kiss
drowning in the hot tongues of sun.

NOAH CREEKMORE
Bingo

Because I have little choice in the matter,
I drive my silent wife downtown.
Stores on the Square burn night lights,
but the movie marquee is brightly lit.
"*Fool's Parade*," I say, my voice rising,
"a real humdinger with Jimmy Stewart."
She says nothing, grips her purse tighter.
We slip past FALSTAFF, WALGREENS, EAT
and turn sharply into South Fifth,
stopping at an ancient red-brick building,
with its scrolled cornices, its roof of pigeons.
The American Legion Hall is where we are,
where the town plays bingo on Tuesday nights.

And the voices are calling back and forth
in the cold-snap September darkness:
"Call me when you're ready, Cary."
"Wish me luck, Wally, lots of good luck."
"Don't spend the food money, Frieda."
Car doors slam, shoes scrape the sidewalk.
My wife nods grimly, says "Same time, Noah."
I drive back toward the empty Square,
in need of male laughter, a dirty joke.
The Courthouse clock is lost in fog.
I pass up EAT and WALGREENS again,
but pull up to the curb at FALSTAFF,
the neon a warm and friendly glow.

POP GAINES
After the Farm Auction

I wanted to bring back some useless thing,
some utterly unusable, used-up thing.
What can you do with a butter churn
that will never churn butter again?
Exactly, you are absolutely correct, old woman.
Nothing, nothing at all.
Go ahead and laugh, make yourself sick.
So I don't know what I'm doing, is that it?
Did I buy the white china doorknob?
Or the emerald-green cathedral relish jar?
Or the Dolly Dingle paper dolls?
Or the mezzotint of St. Francis feeding squirrels?
For old times' sake and for mercy's sake,
no I did not, nor the Boston rocker, either.
The butter churn goes on the kitchen table.
Leave it there, leave it be.
Now then, when is the next farm auction?
I may be needing a coffee grinder next.

YALE BROCKLANDER
Tractor on Main Street

Pay attention while I tell you this.
That beat-up, manure-stained Farmall tractor
you see parked in front of Jake's Tap
is the same Farmall tractor
that was parked in front of the bank yesterday.
Get used to seeing it all over town,
because Tom T. Cassedy won't be put off
just because some lady judge up at the Courthouse
took away his driver's license
for driving drunk into a tree.
Now, a Farmall tractor is not a Lincoln
or even an International pickup,
but as Tom T says, "it's transportation."
He's a persistent cuss, that old coot is.
His face may say "ignorant,"
but his eyes say "devious."
He knows more than one way to get into town
for a snort or two, or three, or four.

BLAKE SAMUELS
Chain Saw

Guess I'll never
learn to keep my
mouth shut. Take for
example last
Saturday when
Dad returned to
his pot roast and
pear salad from
the phone and said,
"That was Lorna.
She said they found
poor Nick out back
of the orchard.
He was dead. He
killed himself with
a chain saw. Right
across the throat.
Unless someone
did it to him,
and they don't think
that's likely," and
I had to say,
"Boy, I'll bet there
was lots of blood.
Lots and lots of
blood." Mother gagged
a bit and smacked
me a good one
upside the head,
and Dad got pissed
real fast and chased
me clear upstairs
into my room
where he shoved me
against the wall,
then slammed the door.
I could hear him
cursing all the
way downstairs to

160

Mother who was
screaming now. Screw
Cousin Nicky.
I hated him.
He was nothing
but a big pain
in the ass and
always kidding
me, nasty-like,
about my not
wanting to kill
and mutilate
wild animals,
and my reading
books all the time,
and why wasn't
a big kid like
me out for the
football team? No,
I'm not sorry
he's dead. But I
have one question
which I'll ask no
one but myself:
"Do you think his
bald head wobbled
off and plopped on
the orchard grass
just like one more
windfall apple?
Do you think that
could have happened
someway, somehow?"

RONALD OSTERLE
Blackboard

I was making noises with Billy.
We were seeing who could sound most
like Donald Duck and Foghorn Leghorn.
My teacher got real mad at me.
She said, "Go up to the blackboard
and write the first ten numbers
we have all been practicing on."
I went to the blackboard and wrote
1 2 3 4 5 6 7 8 10.
My teacher got mad all over again.
She said, "You forgot your 9."
I told her I didn't forget nothing.
I told her that unless she stopped
all that yelling and screaming,
she'd never get any number 9
out of me for her old blackboard.
She said, "You can stay after class."
I told her she couldn't make me.
But she said she could, and she did.
To be a kid is to kid no one.

TIMOTHY PARKER
   Crossing Gates

This girl was on one side
of the railroad tracks
and I was on the other.
We were downtown on Main Street
waiting for a train to go by.
It was a long train,
a mainline freight train
heading west at high noon.
I could catch glimpses of her
in the spaces between the cars.
She was staring at me, too,
a steady straight-ahead look.
I focused on her face at first,
then noticed her crow-black hair,
which was short and very curly.
The cars kept coming,
clanking and swaying and grinding
on their flanged iron wheels.
I took in her legs next.
They looked terrific
in a pair of tight cutoff jeans.
I knew that when the train passed
I would have to speak to her.
The yellow caboose clattered by.
The crossing gates flew up.
We crossed the dusty tracks
toward each other, each other.
"A long, long train," I said.
I glanced at my watch,
a watch that wasn't there.
"Don't be late," she said,
and walked away from me.

FLOYD NYE
  Dog on the Stairs

To live in the second oldest house
in Alliance, Illinois,
is to be aware of many ghosts.
Sometimes late at night,
when a storm is blowing the trees about,
I'll sit up in the big tester bed
and hear the very first man of this place
whisper to his good wife,
who is half-asleep in a lace cap,
"Is that the dog who just went *thump* on the stairs?"
And she'll scratch her right arm and say,
"It's only the wind, Willard."
But I'll get up and go see, anyway,
even though 2:16 a.m. on March 2, 1853,
is a long, long time back,
and the last dog we had
died five years ago this month
under the wheels of a Mayflower van.

DEWEY CLAY DOYLE
Sleeping Bags

We have a resurfaced road smelling ot tar,
a black-eyed susan that escaped the grass fire,
a harp of willow leaves playing the same old tune.

Beyond a field of Shetland ponies cropping red clover,
the morning sun reddens six barn windows.

I have lived around here all my life.

By the yawning mailbox I yawn again
and try to rub the night crumbs from my eyes.
Then when my ride comes along and stops,
I gather up a heavy lunch pail,
a thermos of Susanna's strong coffee,
and *Wild Horse Mesa* by Zane Grey.

Another working day, another day to go to work.

In thirteen minutes I'll be in Alliance
to help make some more sleeping bags.

My name is Dewey Clay Doyle.
You can see it right up there
where I spelled it out with care on the water tank.

LOUISE CATHCART
Hearing an Old Song Again

You don't have to tell me that.
That was "As Time Goes By."
And I know it was a great song
and once warmed up all
the cold kitchens and parlors
in this wind-bitten town.
I used to be happy
as day-old chickens
peeping in a splash of sun-dust
when I'd hear that love tune
on my daddy's new Philco.
But later on it made me sad
because I'd remember the boy
who used to say to me,
his arm around my neck,
"That's our song, lover girl,
and don't you forget it."
Then, just like that,
he moved away to Sioux Falls
and I never saw him again.
That was "As Time Goes By."
You don't have to tell me that.

MARCUS MILLSAP
School Day Afternoon

I climb the steps of the yellow school bus,
move to a seat in back, and we're off,
bouncing along the bumpy blacktop.
What am I going to do when I get home?
I'm going to make myself a sugar sandwich
and go outdoors and look at the birds
and the gigantic blue silo
they put up across the road at Motts'.
This weekend we're going to the farm show.
I like roosters and pigs, but farming's no fun.
When I get old enough to do something big,
I'd like to grow orange trees in a greenhouse.
Or maybe I'll drive a school bus
and yell at the kids when I feel mad:
"Shut up back there, you hear me?"
At last, my house, and I grab my science book
and hurry down the steps into the sun.
There's Mr. Mott, staring at his tractor.
He's wearing his DeKalb cap
with the crazy winged ear of corn on it.
He wouldn't wave over here to me
if I was handing out hundred dollar bills.
I'll put brown sugar on my bread this time,
then go lie around by the water pump,
where the grass is very green and soft,
soft as the body of a red-winged blackbird.
Imagine, a blue silo to stare at
and Mother not coming home till dark!

HAROLD BLISS
Questions and Answers

On my way up to the post office for stamps
I stop awhile in front of the pet store.
Heinz Kleinofen is on a wobbly ladder,
washing his dirty, rain-streaked windows.
"Do you have any rabbits left?" I ask him.
"Bon Ami," he says. "You can't beat it."

Heinz is married to Bertha, a deep thinker
who thinks she looks like Ingrid Bergman.
Surrounded by eighty red teddy bears,
Bertha always lounges in bed till noon.
"How's the good wife these days?" I ask him.
"Swedish," he says. "She can't understand it."

In June, Heinz decides to get far away.
He wants to see the Grand Canyon, alone,
to forget about Bertha and the pet store.
When he returns, I inquire about the trip.
"Did you thrill to the big hole?" I ask him.
"Gila Bend," he says. "I can't believe it."

SAMANTHA TATE
Wet Towels

Say, if I have the cutest ass
on the school volleyball team,
as I've overheard some boys say,
I have the sorest ass also,
because after we became champs again,
me and my teammates went ape shit
in the shower-steamy locker room
and started snapping wet towels
at any pair of bare buns in sight.
We all took a good hit or two,
then for some strange reason the girls
all turned their eyes on me.
They chased me around the room
and long tall Dinah Till grabbed me,
and Heather and Lana held me down
across one of the benches,
and one by one my dear teammates
snapped their towels on my buttocks.
I screamed and cried and cursed them good
before they finally let me go.
They said, "Hey, it was all in fun."
Our coach got real uptight
and said she was ashamed of us.
When the principal heard about it,
he called us into his office
and asked for all the details.
Heather and Lana said it was my fault.
The next day I wore a skirt
instead of my tight jeans to school.
I was walking the hall to English
and this transfer student from Sparta
says to four or five other boys,
"That's got to be the cutest ass
I've seen in a long, long time."
I turned around to face him.
"Oh shut up," I said. "Oh shut up!"

ERIC PECKENPAUGH
Toy Soldiers

Went up to attic and found
box of toy soldiers.
Blue soldiers, red soldiers,
green soldiers, brown soldiers,
soldiers with long rifles,
soldiers wearing gas masks,
soldiers with bayonets,
soldiers riding horses.
Took toy soldiers
down to living room,
slapped their faces,
and threw them in big fire.
Went to get Mama
so she could see
all Daddy's toy soldiers
get burned up real good.
Then went to play outside
and chased my funny dog
with purple hatchet.
Had fun till Mama called me in.

PEARL INGERSOLL
Homework

Three telephone calls,
a chocolate doughnut,
look for lost textbook,
one hour of television,
a pickle, an apple,
Masters's "Petit, the Poet,"
two telephone calls,
a piece of pumpkin pie,
hot bath, shampoo,
Robinson's "Richard Cory,"
Frost's "Fire and Ice,"
a banana, a root beer,
Sandburg's "Chicago,"
another telephone call,
paint toenails red,
Lindsay's "The Congo,"
find lost gym shoes,
corn muffin and milk,
Pound's "Ancient Music,"
Moore's "To a Steam Roller,"
put hair in curlers,
shave legs, brush teeth,
half hour of television,
smoke a Kool cigarette,
Eliot's "Ash Wednesday,"
to bed after midnight.

LUCKY SCHU
A Fool in Love

When the Hong Kong flu hit town
last winter, around Christmas,
I took a direct hit and sank
below the waves of my bed.
I spent two days wanting to die
and one day afraid I would.
The afternoon of the fourth day
I walked the two blocks downtown
to see Doc Heintzelman,
who gave me one of his quick once-overs
and a prescription for some pills.
Then he left the room,
banging the door behind him,
and his nurse came in
with a needle as long
as a cat burglar's rap sheet.
It was Tricia Janacek,
the county sheriff's daughter,
all grown up and plenty cute.
"Drop your pants," she said.
"And your shorts, too."
I did what she said
and she stuck her needle in my buttock.
She never let on she knew me,
from when she lived next door to us
over on River Street.
We had a yellow frame house there,
with a big willow tree
that took up most of the side yard.
One afternoon little Tricia
got her red rubber ball
stuck in the willow branches.
I saw it all from the window
of the dining room where I
was running my Lionel train about.
I climbed up that tree,
quick as a flash,
and knocked her ball down.
I came down quickly, too,

and broke my left wrist,
trying to show off like Tarzan
to my own star -eyed Jane.
"You can dress now," she said.
"Does this mean we're engaged?" I said,
trying to be witty.
"Why, sure, of course.
Let's set the date, too,
while we're at it," she said,
and rolled her pretty eyes
and then left me there
stuffing my shirt into my pants.
So, again, I've played the fool
with the sheriff's daughter.
But, love, love, oh love,
look what you've done to me.
Little Tricia is a big Tricia now.

NELSON HURLBUT
Last Day of Summer Vacation, 1934

The yellow-dog sun rolled over again
as my brother and I, cheeks rosy as peach stones,
galloped cornstalk ponies toward the shady house,
each of us with a corncob gun
going *bang, bang, bang, bang, bang.*

And perched on our mother's grapevined porch
was the third grade teacher fanning her face
with a sumac-red spelling book,
her gray hair swaying like an orchard cobweb,
and she was shouting, "Whoa, horse, slow down there."

Then our deep groans rose up with the dust,
we boys seeing that ancient schoolmarm
brandishing the dreaded speller weapon,
and we dropped corncob guns
and left our limp cornstalk ponies for dead.

STEPHEN FROMHOLD
Freight Trains in Winter

In cheerless December
two trains pass each other
on the empty prairie,
their cars, fired with color
from the going-down sun:
cherry red, pumpkin orange,
corn gold, lima bean green,
two strings of Christmas lights
pulled across the white rug
of a cold winter day,
and all I can say is,
"Let's do it one more time!"

CURLY VANCE
The Pool Players

The tavern is down by the C&NW tracks,
across from Spencer Purdom's grain elevator.
The time is about eleven o'clock
on a snowbound Saturday night.
The pool table is made of northern red oak,
scarred by many railroaders' knives.
But the green felt is good
and the numbered balls run true.
The game is stripes and solids,
or "big balls" versus "little balls."
The menacing black eight-ball is left for last,
when the game is on the line.
The teams are made up of me
and Texaco Cap, from nearby Goodenowville,
shooting against Orange Boots
and that human scarecrow Sycamore Slim.
The stakes are bottles of beer,
the winners collecting after each game.
The other guys drink Pabst Blue Ribbon.
I insist on Grain Belt.
The break is won by our side,
but I can put nothing in any of the pockets.
The balls are spread all over the cloth.
Orange Boots is licking his chops.
The audience consists of two noisy drunks
wearing monogrammed bowling shirts
and a Mexican section-gang worker
who keeps saying, "No, no, don't shoot that one."
The smoke hanging over the table
is from my Washington, Missouri, corncob pipe
and Sycamore Slim's El Productos.
Texaco Cap chews Beech-Nut.
The luck runs all one way.
Sycamore Slim's tricky bank shots
are dropping balls into every pocket.
Texaco Cap is getting hot under the collar,
steaming like a baked potato.
The fight begins when I tell Orange Boots
to lay off banging the overhead light shield

with his goddamned cue stick.
Orange Boots says, "You gonna make me?"
I hit him hard on the side of the head
and Texaco Cap hits him with the nine-ball.
Then there's lots of shoving and wild swinging.
The bartender goes for the telephone.
The cops arrive in no time at all.
Sycamore Slim is last seen
running down the C&NW tracks
with four cold bottles of Pabst Blue Ribbon,
two bags of Beer Nuts, and a Slim Jim.

MISSY UMBARGER
Stories in the Kitchen

The things she'd tell us were things we'd never heard of.

"Missy, you were born at home in a big brass bed.
Yes, a Hampshire boar and two two-horned Dorset lambs.
Karl, my older brother, was the troublemaker.
It was hopscotch, jacks, kick-the-can all summer long.
There is no photograph I know of of Aunt Ruth.
The garage was decorated with license plates.
I'd pick yellow flowers off the cucumber vines.
Ace Van de Vere used to drown himself in bay rum.
Daddy got sore and left Dallas out of the will.
Sister Callie took care of a few red chickens.
We'd go by trolley for a picnic in Barr's woods.
A chili supper in the church basement was great.
The best friend I had was Vida Gum from Beardstown.
Vida it was who gave me this cameo brooch.
Later, Reverend Barnes quit to drive a milk truck.
We'd wade in Logan's Creek holding our long skirts up.
I recall Callie lost Mother's new blue Bible.
Dallas moved to Canada and never came back.
Lordy, you could smell Ace coming a block away.
Our garden went uphill and ran mostly to beans.
The plates were half Wisconsin and half Illinois.
No, Ruth never let Uncle Paul snap her picture.
How I wish I could remember those jump rope rhymes.
Good heavens, Karl went to jail one time for mail fraud.
Right, boars and lambs at a Sons of Norway auction.
Missy, your hair was the color of dry corn shocks."

Grandma Faust was always fun and full of stories.

EUGENE CLARK
Grass Roots

The old lady who told me about
the carved half-moon on the outhouse door
is dead now, dying of kidney failure.
My failure is I didn't ask her
more about hokeypokey Calhoun County,
the county with no railroad tracks.
What I did ask was where she got
those blue suspenders she always wore,
the ones with the playing cards on them.
She said it was none of my business
and banged two Kennedy half dollars on the bar,
yelling for Bernie the friendly barkeep
to give her another beer and a shot.
The old lady who told me about
the carved half-moon on the outhouse door
isn't going to tell me anything new,
and it will no doubt be a long wait
before someone opens up his mouth
in this down-by-the-tracks tavern
and pours out some thrilling stories
concerning the dark and damp provinces
of downstate Illinois, including
up-to-date dope on hog cholera
and yesterday's rain in Prairie du Rocher.

ZOLA THOMAS
The Woman in the Rented Room

Four days before she died,
we heard Miss Teasdale sobbing
in her room down the hall.
We all stopped what we were doing
and glanced at one another
over our books and homework,
spread out on the kitchen table.
"What is she crying about now?"
my brother, Buford, said.
"I'm sure I don't know," I said.
"You'd think she'd be happy it's spring,"
my sister, Starla, said.
"Spring is a fun time," I said.
Mother looked up from darning socks.
Her eyes were red and puffy.
She rapped her thimble on a chair.
"It's time for bed," she said.
That was the end of that.

DALE SUNDBERG
Fir Tree

The fir tree that couldn't stand up straight
is stretched out on the ground now.
I was tired of seeing it so dependent
upon a foot of clothesline to keep it upright,
the rope circling its skinny trunk
and tied to the iron railing of the porch.
I nursed it for five years.
It took just two minutes
to hack it down with a dull Boy Scout hatchet,
the children shouting, "Timber!"
No longer on midwinter mornings
will I have to take the broom
and knock the heavy snow off its branches.
The weather will do it in for good, I thought,
wondering if I would really give a hoot.
What a humpback it was, what a drunken sailor.
I kept hoping that one more year
would make it strong enough
to grow the way it should grow.
But my patience ran out at last.
I found the hatchet behind the woodpile
and did the job as quickly as possible,
feeling sad and relieved at the same time.
"That was fun, Daddy," said my little son.
"Let's chop down another one."

LYNNE MOSEBY
Piano

After supper
the whole family
gathered around
the piano.
We just stood there
and stared at it,
wishing one of us
could play the damn thing.
My dad looked at
his thick farmer's hands
and shook his head.
My little sister
pressed down three keys.
"*Plink, plank, plunk,*" Mom said,
and closed her eyes.
"The piano
is useless," I said.
"It's good for nothing."
So we sold it to
a woman who lived
across town from us
in a big house
and who already
had two pianos,
plus what she called
a harpsichord.

ALAN COMSTOCK
Old Man

I never noticed him much at all:
a housefly bumping against the screen,
a loaf of stale sourdough bread,
a half-dead tree bending over a brown river.
But my grandpa was there, always there,
and when now and then he would call from the kitchen,
"You care to share a mushroom omelette?"
I would holler, "In a minute, Gramps,"
and then go and eat with him.
We seldom said a word to each other.
He was backward. I was mostly bored.
When he died last month in an ambulance,
after another paralyzing stroke,
we spread his things on the bed:
two gray suits, a worn-out Elgin watch,
a diploma from a Vermont trade school.
I salvaged his copies of the *Police Gazette*
and an unused pair of Nunn-Bush shoes.
No one talks about Grandpa these days.
I don't remember him much at all.

JUDY WYCKOFF
Howling Walter

The dog's name was Walter.
He howled and howled so much,
we called him "Howling Walter."
He couldn't do a damn thing but howl,
and he did that all day long.
Since the dog wasn't ours to straighten out
we went about our business,
not wanting to create a fuss
and have another fuss come back at us
when we did something our neighbor
wasn't going to sit still for.
We knew that sooner or later
old Howling Walter would get his, but good.
And he did, late last night
while howling at a Sinclair oil truck,
which ran him over on School Street.
None of us said we were sorry.
And no one said we should be.

184

MARTY HUBBARD
Four Bottles of White Wine

"I hope the girls get here soon," I said,
and pulled back the skin on a bruised banana.
Al took out a shiny Ace pocket comb
and ran it through his thining hair.
Buddy Rich's *Very Live at Buddy's Place*
boomed from Al's new K-Mart stereo.
We finished a can of Vienna sausage
and started in on some onion rings.
"You should ditch this horsehair sofa," I said.
"Sit on the floor you don't like it," Al said.
"This is one scratchy old couch," I said.
The telephone rang and Al answered with,
"Shapiro's All-Night Massage Parlor."
When he put down the receiver, I asked him,
"Who was that? Who was that calling?"
"I don't know, they hung up," Al said.
Soft, rich, and intimate, the summer wind
pushed up from the sticky southland.
It billowed the white lace curtains
and blew some ashes off the ashtray.
A Ford convertible stopped at the curb.
Two girls got out with four bottles of white wine
and an economy-size bag of corn chips.
"Who's that on tenor sax?" I said.
"Sal Nistico," Al said, and opened the door.
"Party time," one of the girls said.
"Hello, hello, it's about time," I said,
and reached for a bottle of Blue Nun.

BOOTH SCHOFIELD
  A Dream of Old

In this old and done-for town
all the trees and streets are old,
and the stores and houses are old.
The men and women are thin, bent, and old.
They sit on dilapidated front porches
in their very oldest old clothes
and either read old almanacs and old books
or just rock in old rocking chairs,
staring into old fading-quilt sunsets
until it is time to disappear behind old doors.
I recall stopping here in the old days
at the old stone hotel on Old Mill Street
and hearing nothing but old jokes and stories
drifting like clouds of stale tobacco smoke
over the dusty ferns in the overheated lobby.
I left muttering old oaths, feeling old myself.
Now, on this old river-fog morning,
I have returned, my curiosity rising again,
my memories turning like an old Ferris wheel,
to find the old courthouse has collapsed.
With my cane I poke about in the rubble
that is spread across the Square.
An old Mathew Brady photograph of General Grant
falls through an old and burnt-out sun.

Anyway, at least the children here are not old,
even if they do have old and sad eyes,
sing old railroad songs with old faraway voices,
and play games of tag in old side yards
among old dogs and old pussy cats.
I want to befriend them, to get to know them.
I shake a boy's hand and it crumbles to dust.
A girl in old calico has flies caked to her nose.
What is this all about? What have I done?
Startled, I scream, then I begin to weep.
The children's faces spring to old smiles.
They quickly drop old balls and old dolls
and run off like chickens in a storm
to climb old locked and rusty gates.

Sure, I know what old tricks they are up to.
They are hell-bent in scampering to old attics,
hoping to find their old Halloween masks,
which are buried deep in old steamer trunks.
You see, they don't want an old coot to think
that they too can't be old and funny.
Oh why is it always, always the children,
blessed with an old, old wisdom,
who will try hardest to please
an old and foolish stranger?

CANDY MIZEROCK
Blues Alphabet

This long morning I
was all alone and
put sad songs on the
record player, for
I wanted to see
if I could shed some
new nostalgic tears
and write a few words
I thought were true, but
the music and the
songs were too full of
thorny memories,
and I jotted down
nothing but sweet and
sour lies as a cold
wind blew in from the
apple orchard and
spoiled fruit rolled across
the goodbye grass, and
it was just no use,
I was stuck with my
blues alphabet, my
tricky grammar of
twig-snapped yesterdays,
and I gloomed out the
dusty bay window
until the music
and the songs were done.

188

NETTIE KERSHAW
Pickle Puss

Moody?
Him?
Cyrus ?
No.
He's never
in a good mood.
Great balls of fire,
what a grouch
my brother is.
Glum isn't the word,
nor crabby, either.
A tiny smile
would crack his face,
but you'd wait
a whole heap longer
than Judgment Day
to see one.
Moody?
Moody?
Don't make me laugh.
Cy hasn't had
a good day
since he swallowed
a chew of Red Man
behind Pop's barn,
and that
was some sixty-odd
years ago.
Moody?
No.
Never.
Not
Pickle Puss.

OSCAR CHEATHAM
Scotch Pine

This year we decide to go out to a farm where they let you cut down your own Christmas tree. So here we are, deep in the cornfields, standing around in an apple-cider shed, drinking apple cider and shooting the breeze with the farmer and the farmer's daughter, who has quickly captured the lustful eye of my son. "About time to go bag us a good-looking tree," I say. "Yes, I think we'd better get to it before it gets dark," my wife says. "Plenty of time," my son says, his undivided attention focused on the farm girl's more than ample bosom and tight jeans. "Every tree here is fifteen dollars, no matter how large or how small," the farmer says. "Does that include those big maple trees over there by the house?" I say. Everyone has a good laugh and we help ourselves to more apple cider from the tap. The heady aroma of ripe and overripe apples is beginning to make me giddy. "Try to cut the tree not more than two inches above the ground," the farmer says, handing me a saw. "Let's go," my wife says. "Okay," I say, and we put down our cider cups and head out across the corn stubble-field toward a thick stand of scotch pine. "Pretty sunset," my wife says. "I love it here," I say. "Ah, yes, the good life in the sweetest little rural crotch in all of Sunflower County," my son says. The kid is starting to sound more and more like his old man, much to the dismay of his mother, who glares at me, not him.

ROMA HIGGINS
Cricket

For a whole week
there was a cricket
in the cellar,
somewhere between
the furnace
and the croquet set.
I would go down
every evening
to hear him chirp.
He would note my steps
and break off
his magic music.
Then he would begin
to sing again.
It got so
I would talk to him
and call him friend.
But tonight
in the cellar
I found nothing
but cold silence
and a spider
working on a shroud
by the window.

AVERY LUCAS
   Apples

It's that time of year again,
so I grab my walnut cane
and take my string bag
off the hall closet hook
and walk down Grant Street
under a blowing rain
of yellow and russet leaves.
I pass a dozen boys playing
football on a muddy lawn,
pass sumac and grapevine,
pass front porch steps
orange with pumpkins,
pass smoking leaf piles,
pass Feldkamp's lumberyard
which smells of redwood planks,
pass the empty public pool,
pass the first farm west
where a monstrous corn picker
harvests a forest of corn,
and then come at last
to an abandoned orchard
of six scrawny trees.
Here, I gather the ugliest
apples you've ever seen:
puny, lopsided, bird-pecked,
yet possessing a special
flavor all their own.
And no one knows this,
no one except me, Avery Lucas,
and I'm not telling nobody
nothing about nothing.

DELBERT VARNEY
One-Way Conversation with a Rug Beater

Bam, bam, bam went the baseball bat.

Her pa was out in back beating a rug for his wife.
He had a neck like a wrestler and hair in his ears.
I sat on the lawn and chewed a blade of grass.
"Did you know I'm in love with your daughter?" I said.

Bam, bam, bam went the baseball bat.

The dust really jumped from that sad old rug.
He had a tattooed chest and a scar on his left cheek.
I sat on the porch and smoked a Lucky Strike.
"Did you hear I'm marrying your daughter?" I said.

Bam, bam, bam went the baseball bat.

KARL THEIS
The Widower Turns Eighty

Old November is novembering again.

Now whose blind and broken dog
is sprawled in that heap of brown leaves?

Somewhere beyond those dead elms
a pale woman calls my name,
but she doesn't mean me, no, not me,
for my name disappeared years ago
in a rush of November wind,
about the time I had my first stroke
and the last Burma Shave sign
was ripped out like a vile weed
on the southern edge of Sunflower County.

My body is a cracked cornstalk.
My face is dusted with crop dust.

November again and again and again.

SHELLEY BROWN
Acorns

I was over at Olin's house for a half hour or so.
He's a big-time acorn collector now,
having given up seashells and matchbook folders,
having thrown in the towel on beer cans.
Any old kind of acorn will do him.
He's not a bit persnickety, not that boy,
any more than your average ground squirrel is.
His bedroom is under siege to an acorn army.
There are acorns stockpiled in chairs,
on shelves, on his bureau, on windowsills,
plus battalions of acorns all over the rug,
not to mention in shoe boxes and coffee cans,
even a disorderly platoon of them on the bed.
I will try not to tell you that I think he's nuts,
because I'd be caught with a bad joke.
Still, one wonders what's going on in that head,
the head that put his name on the honor roll
his first three years at Alliance High School.
When I left, he put an acorn in my hand.
"Put this in a safe place," he said.
"It's going to be a long, cold winter."

CHARLEY HOOPER
Schoolteacher

Barefoot in the sticky June twilight,
I mow a patch of stone-jumping grass.
The girl next door makes a sick, throw-up face
and stirs her drum of burning trash.
Across the street the retired switchman
hawks and spits on a ramshackle porch.
My son, a dirty diaper around his knees,
offers me one lick of his dripping ice cream cone.
I find a moldy tennis ball near the doghouse
and bounce it off old Butler's roof.
A big decision must be made soon,
grade arithmetic papers? or drink some booze?
There have been many nights like tonight,
many hours of what to do? where to go?
And wouldn't you just know this too:
the Dodge Charger has another flat tire!

MILO FERRIS
A Damned Pretty Rain

With his stained and shapeless hat
shoved way back on his head,
Cleghorn was telling us there was doom
if it didn't rain soon—today,
tonight, this very weekend, now.
"The corn will dry up and you'll see
what you'll be paying for steak,
pot roast, chops, and hamburger."
We all nodded, said, "Sure, Cleghorn,"
and went our separate ways,
still nodding, toward drugstore,
toward tavern, toward Courthouse.
And in two days it rained hard,
and it rained hard for two days:
lightning, thunder, downpour, deluge.
Now, a couple of days later,
we see Cleghorn coming up from the bank.
"I got me some Grade A troubles,"
he says, pushing his hat back.
"Corn is all washed out on my land.
What do I need a dozen lakes for?"
"It was a damned pretty rain,"
I tell him, real nice, all smiles.
Hutchinson winks at McCarthy
and McCarthy elbows Hutchinson.
Cleghorn spits on the sidewalk
and jams the dirty hat over his eyes.
"Damned pretty rain, my ass!" he says,
and stalks off toward his truck.

LYLE MURPHY
Pregnant

Freida wouldn't tell her father
I was the one got her pregnant.
"He'll kill you for sure," she said.
I knew his temper, his fits of violence.
"But he'll get it out of you," I said.
"He won't let you be until he does."
So I went over to her house last night
and told him I was the guy that did it.
"Damn it, we both got stupid," I said.
He just stared at me, bared his smoky teeth,
and knocked the news across his knee.
You'll never know how relieved I was.
Then her mother walked into the room,
twisting a dish towel in her hands,
and she slapped me off the davenport
and beat me with her tiny fists.
"Look, I'll marry her," I said quickly.
But she kicked me hard in the groin
and filled my ears with, "You bastard!"
"Mothers," I said, "little old mothers,"
and I limped toward the screen door.

TERRY REESE
  Boom Boom on B Street

It was the two feet of snow that did us in.
Man, what a blizzard that baby was.
Lois, eyes hard as icicles, kept saying
she was finished with me, kaput,
was going home to Mother, getting out for good.
"Bitch, bitch, bitch, bitch, bitch," I said,
as I had been saying for weeks and weeks,
knowing we were cracking up this winter,
what with all the snow, the goddamn snow,
piling up everywhere you'd care to look,
and that our marriage had dropped below zero.
"You can keep the dog," she said.
"I hate him more than I hate you."
What an urge I had to knock her on her can.
"But I'm taking the car," she said.
I said nothing, but got out the shotgun.
She followed me outside, without her coat or hat,
the icy wind whipping her hair about.
I tell you I must have been off my nut,
about good and ready for a rubber room.
I pumped four shells into that old Oldsmobile:
the windshield, both front tires,
then lifted up the snow-capped hood
and put a blast in the carburetor.
Lois screamed and hugged the dog.
"Not him, oh not him, too," she said.
I stumbled toward her, falling once, twice,
and we tumbled in the snowbank.
Then we cried and cried, all the frozen tears
dripping down like a bad leak in the roof.
"It's snowing again," she said at last.
"We're not going anyplace," I said.
I tossed the shotgun in the wrecked car
and kissed the dog on his runny nose.

CASEY DIXON
Moony

When she's acting
moony around
the farm and looks
way off someplace
like she sees a
buzzard wearing
a pair of gold
earrings, she talks
to the cats and
the dog and the
chickens in the
chicken coop and
to sweet corn and
pumpkins and squash
out there in the
garden plot and
to the hammock
in the yard and
the rocking chair
on the front porch
and to all the
cars and pickup
trucks that zip by
blowing up dust,
and for Pete's sake
even to the
dirty dishes
stacked like bad dreams
in the sink and
the mop and the
oven and the
washing machine
and the potted
fern we got in
the dining room,
and I'm so darn
tired of saying,
"Hey, what is wrong
with you today,
Anna Marie?"

and not getting
back a single
word like she don't
know me from old
Moses, and if
I ask her when
supper will be
ready, she takes
a can of pork
and beans off the
shelf and sets it
on the kitchen
table and she
means if I want
to eat, there it
is, and I go
out the screen door
and walk slowly
to the barn and
kick dirt clods and
a couple of
little bitty
red corncobs and
curse the fate of
being hitched to
a country girl
with moony spells.

ALICIA JACKSON
Fire Dream

The fire
destroyed
everything
I owned,
everything
except
the clothes
I was wearing
and a new
poem
I had cooking
in my head,
a poem
about
a fire
destroying
everything
I owned,
everything
except
the clothes
I was wearing
and a new
poem
I had cooking
in my head.

IRWIN STREETER
Worms

"You don't have any bait? No bait?"

We get in the car and take off,
driving deep into the farm country
of northern Illinois.
We watch the signs, all kinds of signs.
Signs everywhere, signs
saying EGGS,
saying RAILROAD CROSSING,
saying NUTRENA FEEDS,
saying KEEP GATE CLOSED,
saying SWEET CORN,
saying ROAD WORK AHEAD,
saying BABY KITTENS,
saying TOMATOES AND BEANS,
saying DO NOT PASS,
saying SPEED LIMIT 55,
saying COUNTY LINE ROAD,
saying FUNK'S G-HYBRID,
saying CUCUMBERS,
saying NARROW BRIDGE,
saying FOR SALE BY OWNER,
saying LEMONADE,
saying BEWARE OF DOG,
saying WATCH FOR CHILDREN,
saying NO HUNTING,
saying DEAD END.
Then, at last, we find it,
a homemade sign nailed to an oak tree
saying WORMS.

"Now, son, you can go fishing again."

HARLAN ADCOCK
Body

The dead man in my October cornfield
should have run off quick to Switzerland,
is not in shape to hunt pheasants,
lies on his side, his hands tied,
wears cuff links the size of door knockers,
has frosty-morning whiskers, rusty teeth,
won't do for fertilizer,
can't pull up his socks or tuck in his shirt,
looks a good bit like Pretty Boy Floyd,
doesn't hear the caw of crows,
will miss the Army-Navy game,
could be a gangster from Chicago,
was shot once in the head, twice in the heart.

GERTRUDE VON ERICH
School Board

Three times now
I have failed to be elected
in a school board election,
and it's surely not because my last name
is Prussian
but because
I stood right up and said our needy schools
should be given more money
and should teach the children Chinese
and Russian.

I see I'm rhyming again,
rhyming again,
a childish habit,
better left to sad and silly poets
or Hallmark cards.
Nevertheless,
my sneering townspeople,
the death of defeat
is the same old verse,
the same cold bottom line.

FRED DELOPLAINE
   Illinois Farmers

We are waiting to plant corn.

Not yet
too wet
not yet
too wet
not yet
too wet
not yet
too wet
not yet
too wet
not yet
too wet
not yet
too wet.

We are waiting to plant corn.

EDWINA McBRIDE
Trademarks

Dear old Daddy was always very precise:
"The shovel is out by the Cyclone chain-link fence."
"We've run out of Glad plastic garbage bags."
"Buy Tabasco pepper sauce and Kodachrome film."
"I'm going to need more of that Sheetrock gypsum wallboard."
"Get your feet off my Naugahyde vinyl-coated chair."
Daddy has been gone close to eight weeks now.
He's up there in that all-American trademark heaven,
telling the boys all about Prestone antifreeze,
Univac computers, Neolite soles and heels,
and the pure wisdom of using Scotchgard stain repeller.
But Mom is still here, bless her vague little heart:
"'Edwina, honey, put away those kitchen doodads."
"Try on that new pink whatchamacallit I bought for you."
"I can't have your thingamajigs laying around."
"Where's that doohickey I left on the hall table?"
"We must look nice for my friend Miss Whoozis."
Daddy, Daddy, she's driving me crazy.
I just have to straighten out this nameless wife of yours.
She doesn't know it and she'll never know it,
but she's gotten out the Q-Tips cotton swabs,
Niblets corn, and the Electrikbroom vacuum cleaner.

207

AARON FICKLIN
Brother

This is Halloween night, Andy.
The ghosts and goblins are going about,
costumed kids with their tricks and treats,
with their sacks full of candy and apples.
But I'm here, drinking from a pint of Antique,
the bourbon with the train on the label,
and gazing down at your moonlit headstone:
QUENTIN ANDREW FICKLIN
1949—1974
A cold wind is pouring stiff leaves
through the tall tree of heaven.
I smell frost and pine needles and weeds.
Oh, I feel sort of stupid coming to this place,
and, yes, a little phony too.
Still, I do like these country graveyards.
They are always so full of crazy names
and sad angels with broken wings.
Listen, boy, no one blames me for shooting you.
Just an accident, they say.
It can happen, will happen, does happen.
Not that that changes things, of course.
Well, Andy, brothers we were, sure,
but never, ever, friends, I guess.
And, if anything, being drunk as a skunk,
that's what devils me good tonight.
Hey, we sold your law books last week,
and we got a pretty fair price for them,
considering they were so beat up and all.
We hope the stamps and coins will go next.
You won't care, will you, Andy?
Boy, the other news isn't much.
Poor Bernice has got pimples real bad
and stays in her room day after day
plunking, just plunking, your blues guitar.
Dad is grouchy and is growing a beard.
Mom is silent as a slab of cheese.
But this, this is what you should know:
I aim to hunt only with loud strangers now.
Bang. Yell. Shout. Pheasants! Bang. Bang. Bang.

208

Brother, the Courthouse clock strikes ten.
I'm fixing to move away in your old boots.
They fit, boy. They're my new drinking boots.
The bottle's empty. All gone. Drunk up.
I'm going. I'm walking. I'm running.
Lord, Lord, the restless, relentless moon
stalks me through a death of black corn.

MAX VERDERBER
Ausagaunaskee

The Ausagaunaskee River possesses a nice piece of the summer sky. It has always been that way. The river pulls the sky down and holds on passionately, one proud lover joining another proud lover. At sunset, the sky sings out of a ruby-red throat. The river also sings out of a ruby-red throat, taking the sky's great flaming mouth to its broad breast. When darkness comes, in the cool green of the evening, when all the river's trees are heavy with the sky's birds, the Ausagaunaskee and the summer sky get lost in each other, rolling over and over and over on each other. Something very similar to the above also happens in fall, winter, and spring. There could be many river and sky songs written about this.

BETSY PETTIGREW
Carnival on Eye Street

The two-bit,
three-day carnival
they have every August
in this one-horse town
is set up again
on the same weedy lot
at the end of Eye Street.
And we are going
to the carnival,
as we always do,
but not for the fun of it,
not to eat cotton candy,
not to shoot metal ducks,
not to see the tractor pull,
and most certainly
not to ride the merry-go-round.
No, we keep going back
year after year
to win us a new car.
And this year
we got six tickets
on a Ford Thunderbird,
and if we win,
Pappy says
I can learn to drive,
if I don't think sixty
is too old to learn how.

JEROME HOLTSAPPLE
Flower Thief

Mrs. Stockton must have seen me from where
she sat swinging on the front porch swing.
"What you doing picking my flowers?" she said.
"I just took one red marigold," I said.
"Well what you want it for?" she said.
"It's—it's for my girlfriend," I said.
That was a lie, for I picked it for me.
"You're a little too old for that stuff," she said.
I wanted to say something real smart
or roll my eyes like Groucho Marx,
but I couldn't do it, couldn't pull it off.
"I might ring up the sheriff," she said.
"You do that now," I said, getting mad.
"A real wise guy, ain't you?" she said.
"Here's something else to get sore about," I said,
and pulled the petals off three white roses.

KEVIN PRUITT
Taking Down the Flag

We're fifth graders now,
so all of us kids are grown old enough
to take down the flag after school.
The first afternoon, I told Freddie:
"Don't let it touch the ground.
Don't let it touch the ground.
Don't let it touch the ground."
But he let it touch the ground.
Freddie let the flag touch the ground.
I told him over and over:
"Don't let it touch the ground."
But it weren't no use,
so I kicked him hard in the butt
and called him a bad word.
I don't know why they got mad on me.
It weren't me let the flag touch the ground.

CLYDE ROCKWELL
Bus Stop

Before the thundershower,
I stared for a long, long time
at a pig-plump waitress,
waiting for her evening bus.

Corn tasseled in my groin.
My hands ripened to melons.

I'll farm where I damn please.

RACHEL OSGOOD
Cornhusk Dolls

A warm dream of little girls
playing with cornhusk dolls
on the porch of a country house,
the sun falling in dusty slants
through a tangle of sweet-pea vines,
female chitchat and laughter,
washed and ironed cotton dresses
hugging the rough doll bodies.

Then the dream breaking up
when I awake to midwinter sleet
drumming against the windowpanes,
and again I must live without
a daughter, a worried child
who whispers sweetly in my ear,
"Have you seen my pretty dolly?
I think I left her in the corn."

PATRICIA WELLS
Picking the Garbage

It's all out there on the curb,
everything we don't want,
and here come the people.
There goes the paint-stained table
with the wobbly legs.
The guy limping on a cane got it.
His son grabs the Virgin Mary statue
Vern had in the Omega.
Cute little tot wants Lou's tricycle.
Her father is shaking his head,
but her mother disagrees with him,
says to bring it along.
Look at that woman there, in the green hat,
looking over the stack of books.
She takes eleven paperbacks
back to the Plymouth Duster
and drives down the street.
Now the lamp Ed made in the eighth grade
is snatched up by a black girl
wearing a Michael Jordan shirt.
The homemade parrot perch goes next
and the plastic pineapple
Aunt Pearl sent us from Hawaii.
Four old record albums disappear
and three tires, two lawn chairs.
It's the annual cleanup day
and half the town, it seems,
is out picking the garbage.

NED SWIFT
Downtown

Anything going on downtown, you ask?
You better believe it, my good friend.
The mail truck got in early
but went out late,
there's another huge pothole
right in front of the Mobil station,
the Grain Belt beer sign at Jake's
was wrecked sometime last night,
and a Funk's G-Hybrid seed salesman
and a retired pharmacist
from Prophetstown, Illinois,
were hammering out a new foreign policy
on the stone bench at the Courthouse.
But that's not all,
that's not the half of it.
Up at the Dairy Queen,
Jennifer Hornbeck told me
that she wouldn't speak to me again
unless I got rid of my shoes,
my jeans, and my T-shirt that says
It Takes Leather Balls to Play Rugby.
Now, my question is:
Does she want me naked tonight
after the band concert in the Square?

ANTHONY FASANO
  Greenhorn

It was the pinball that did it,
how I went from nobody to somebody
at Harry Peacock's hardware store.
I started off pretty bad there.
I didn't fall for the left-handed monkey wrench,
but they got me with the striped paint.
Naturally I became "the greenhorn"
and had to listen to comic remarks like
"You still living in that three-story house
over that vacant lot on Union Street?"
When the lunch hour rolled around
I could hardly wait to get out of there,
to get away from the make-fun-of-the-dago jokes.
I'd go across the Square and play pinball:
ga-ga-ga-ga, goin-goin-goin-goin,
ga-ga-ga-ga, goin-goin-goin-goin.
It got to be a real obsession with me,
this playing pinball all the time.
After supper, with no one to see or be with,
I'd go into one tavern after another
and play game after game after game.
My scores got higher and higher.
I was working the flippers to perfection,
slapping the machine to coax the silver ball
into the more productive pockets,
and the numbers kept jumping on the scoreboard.
When I started winning bonus games
I knew I was ready for blood.
Yeah, I was good, and then some.
I could do everything but make those machines talk.
Then the bums at the store heard about it
and said they could take my ass
anytime, anyplace, and no fooling.
Well, they came around and they tried,
but I beat every one of them and no fooling.
I beat Dennis, Glenn, and Irving
on every pinball machine in Sunflower County.
I killed them on the Flying Chariots,

218

murdered them on the Buckaroo,
flattened them on the King of Diamonds,
and destroyed them on the Abra Ca Dabra.
"Hey," Irving said, "is this really Tony Fasano,
our own little hardware store greenhorn?"
I shoved another coin in the Abra Ca Dabra,
pulled back the plunger, and let the ball fly.
I didn't want to talk to them anymore.
All I wanted were the musical sounds of
ga-ga-ga-ga, goin-goin-goin-goin,
ga-ga-ga-ga, goin-goin-goin-goin
and maybe all night and maybe forever.

CRYSTAL GAVIS
Depressed After Being Fired from Another Job

The black ant drags a bread crumb
clear across the kitchen floor.

That's something else I can't do.

URBIE TUCKER
Wild Asparagus

I was told to stay
in the truck
and not make a fuss.
My pa said
he and Ma and Fletch
would be back
before very long,
or sooner
if they failed to find
something called
wild asparagus.
I always
have to stay behind
when they go
traipsing off somewhere.
Okay, I've
waited long enough.
When they get
back to where I was,
I'll be gone.
I'll be looking for
pieces of
colored glass, bent nails,
and neat stuff
like old radios
and car parts
that people call junk.
I'm going
to spend all my life
collecting
what nobody wants.
Beats me what's
so doggone special
about this
wild asparagus,
anyhow.

L. D. McDOWELL
Apprentice Plumber

We fixed a clogged kitchen sink
and a high-water toilet at Grimms'.
"You're no good for plumbing,"
he said to me, back in the truck,
slipping some Skoal between lip and gum.
I had fumbled through my first week
trying to learn the plumber's trade.
I thought it would be a real pipe,
if you'll please excuse the poor pun.
"You're no good for plumbing,"
he said again as we drove off.
"You can't let the smells get to you,
or the old ladies hanging around,
making you sore with their bum advice."
"I'm no good for plumbing,"
I said, shaking my head sadly.
"That's right," he said. "That's right.
You're not the plumbing type at all.
Stick to writing those poems.
You're a rhymer, not a reamer."

BECKY FARMER
Seen and Not Heard

My brother he's four years old today
and I'm going on eight and a half.
We're not supposed to talk to any strangers,
but did you drop this here tomato?
We saw it laying on your grass
and wondered if you coulda dropped it.
Or maybe you threw it out,
seeing it was kinda small and yellow,
and you couldn't, wouldn't eat it that way.
I know that my brother here,
who like I say is four years old today,
won't eat nothing that's yellow,
although he ate a sorta yellow tomato
that we had for supper tonight.
But he never said a word against it,
'cause Mom and Dad they got this rule
that kids should be seen and not heard,
and if you have that same rule,
you are maybe getting mad with us
for talking to you in your yard.
So I think I'd better grab my brother
and roll him home in his wagon real quick
and let you decide about the tomato:
if it's yours or not yours
and if you think it's too yellow to eat yet.

HERSCHEL NIEDERCORN
Requiem

Aunt Pauline was a bright lights girl,
the kind who likes hotel lobbies, noisy bars,
opera night, New Year's Eve on State Street,
and a steak approximately the size of a doormat.
When she knew she had only a short time to live,
we brought her out to the country:
muddy roads, bare locust trees, frozen lawns,
a barn full of Holstein cows, lots of kids.
She stayed in the house all winter,
telling us stories about her many travels,
playing hearts and dominoes, reading Sherlock Holmes.
By spring, she had lost a lot of weight,
and I knew the worst was soon to come.
We took one last ride in the Dodge pickup,
waved to the rowdy Callison girls
singing "Rock of Ages" on their screened porch,
stopped by the creek, watched the squirrels play.
Tonight she kissed Benjy, our youngest boy,
who said, "I can belch anytime I want to."
She died upstairs in the sewing room.
She said, "I touched the sun on a red flower
and it was cold, so terribly cold."
Aunt Pauline was a bright lights girl.

TERESA BIRDSELL
Sunflower Queen

It was not the blue ribbon I wanted,
not a token to hang in the kitchen,
but just the knowing I was best,
to be tops at something for once,
some success to remember a day by,
to have a day worth remembering.
So when I won first prize
for the biggest sunflower
at the Sunflower County Fair,
I knew I had all I really wanted,
that I needed no loud praise,
no handshakes, no bear hugs,
no snapshots to paste in a book,
nor even a freckled nephew's
"Grandma's the new sunflower queen."

I picked up my handsome champion
and kissed it the way a mother
would kiss an exceptional child,
and I patted its stiff dry head,
recalling a lost cornhusk doll.
Then I walked out into the sun,
past food tent and Ferris wheel,
and right out of the fairgrounds,
moving through rings of gnats,
crying with strange jubilation,
at peace with the cockeyed world,
at ease with myself at last.
When I came to the crossroads,
I stopped, dried my eyes,
and went back to get my sunflower.

SCOOTER HARGROVE
Punch Bowl

Grandpa said he was too
weak and shaky to climb
on a stool and get his
cut-glass heirloom punch bowl
and would I be a good
boy and get it down for
him, and I got on the
stool and reached up to the
top shelf and was bringing
it down like he said when
it slipped out of my hands
and busted into a
thousand little pieces
and he said, "It appears
you are weak and shaky
too and there will be no
punch now so scoot out the
door and play with the dog
if you can manage to
do that," and I got nipped
on the wrist by his bitch
hound while trying to snatch
a stick away from her,
and I won't go back to
my grandpa's house again
even if Ma and Pa
pay me a dime a day
until they've gone busted.

JEFFREY KOHRS
Summer Employment

I don't want to clean out stables.
I don't want to detassel corn.
I don't want to bag groceries.
I don't want to wash dishes.
I don't want to mow cemetery grass.
I want to do what Dad did
when he was sixteen years old.
I want to spend my summer
under a '57 Chevy.
Did you hear me correct?
That's what I want to do.
I want to spend my summer
under a '57 Chevy.
"Oh, dry up," my sister says.
"You're going to work like the rest of us."
Mom says nothing, just bites her lip.
Dad isn't around, of course.
You know where old Dad is, right?
Sure you do. You bet you do.
Okay, all together now:
"He's out there in the side yard
under a '57 Chevy."

BOOG MONCRIEF
Falling Apart

The eleven o'clock freight horns through town
and creeps across the rusted iron bridge.

Dad's abandoned mill shudders in its bones.
Windows shake at Guthrie's Feed and Grain.

I wait patiently behind crossing gates,
my head full of bedpans and blood tests.

That birch tree there at the side of Bliss Road
will never make another green leaf.

No more wet dreams, few erections, no pep,
no lust for that cute county health nurse.

This ruined sidewalk crumbles to sidewalk dust.
A blind man pokes his cane in the weeds.

Hey, you want to know something funny, Faye?
I think I'm a bit too old for you.

PAUL SUMMERHAY
Manuscript

For the best reason I know, namely,
that I don't want to talk about it,
discuss it, go over it, argue about it.
It's no more than that, that's all.
Some things are better left unsaid.
And I know you don't want to hear the news,
because it's not good news for you,
and it certainly hasn't been good for me.
Okay, I'll quit stalling around now.
It wasn't Quinlan's manuscript I left there,
in the big, bad cathouse in Chicago,
it was your manuscript I left there,
the collection of stories and poems.
And I can't go back there to retrieve it
because I forget where that place was, is.
All those Chicago streets look alike,
especially in the dark, when you're drunk.
So what can I do? Where can I turn?
I know what you can do, must do:
blow up, call me names, even punch me out.
Lord knows, Al, I deserve it, in spades.
I read through half of your manuscript,
up to where the eccentric beekeeper
throws a hive of bees into the squad car.
You write well, or at least not bad,
but I do wish you had made yourself a carbon
or saved some drafts, or something.
Look, cheer up, look on the bright side.
Maybe one of those good cathouse ladies,
out of the goodness of her cathouse heart,
will show it to some big-time publisher,
some bird just in from the East Coast
in need of some Windy City tail.

GRETCHEN NAYLOR
Cloakrooms

"Let me go. I'm late to class," he said.

"All the poorly-lit cloakrooms
at Emerson grammar school
smell of soaked oilskin raincoats,
slick-slimy oilskin rain hats,
soggy paper-sack lunches,
and a few heads of wet hair,"
I said to this rabbit-faced kid,
who wiggled his snub nose.

"What are you talking about?" he said.

"Boy, it's been raining, raining,
pouring all day and all night.
Monday, Tuesday, now Wednesday.
It always rains in the fall.
Maybe you're dumb or something.
You better repeat fourth grade,"
I said to this rabbit-faced kid,
who bit me on the arm.

"I'm only in third grade now," he said.

DENNY GRIMES
Winged Seeds

Still breathing hard, still trembling,
I stand under the sugar maple
and hold on to the frayed rope that held up
the rubber tire we used to swing on.
It was nice having that tire here.
We swung often, even in midwinter,
when we were sick of parents and stuffy rooms.
I look at leaves and clouds.
Winged seeds, like little toy propellers,
spin down to the ground.
I pick one up, look at it,
then slip it carefully into my shirt pocket.
My sister Francie slams the front door
and runs toward Second Street again.
This morning I heard her shout,
"I hate you, Mom. I hate you. I hate you!"
Francie always runs away when she's angry.
Clouds drift across the noonday sun.
Maple leaves shake in the damp wind.
Why did I do it? Why?
I was almost finished making a model plane.
Tired from bending over my desk,
and getting a headache from smelling glue,
I went to the bathroom to get a drink of water.
"My god," I said. "My god!"
Two more pimples had erupted on my face,
and the big spring dance just five days off.
I couldn't stand it, I tell you.
I slammed the plastic cup on the floor
and stamped out of there in a red rage.
That's when I smashed
my De Havilland DH-4 Light Bomber.
Boy, did the balsa wood go flying.
Francie and I have had our problems here.
And where is my shoe box of colored stones,
my envelope of winged seeds?

KERRY WOODRUFF
  Nicolette

My lively lover,
lovely muscled,
squirming with love,
rolls a moist thigh
over my belly
after we make love.
Beyond the split-rail fence
there are oodles
and oodles
of sweet red raspberries
that want to be picked.
But Nicolette wants
to stay awhile,
to make more love,
the rhythms
of our loins
throbbing in the heat
of this midday daybed.
She closes her eyes
and a perfect poem
ripens between
raspberry tits.

JUDGE EMIL ZANGWILL
Angry Words

It's Friday night again in Alliance, Illinois.
I leave the Courthouse by the jail-side door.
I'm drained from endless bickerings of the courtroom,
the lies, the tears, the bloodlust accusations,
sick of sharp-tongued lawyers and dull-eyed juries.
On my way home, walking toward Liberty Street,
I stop at Bert and Larry's liquor store
to pick up a quart of Jack Daniel's black label,
then continue to plod along for another two blocks,
the April mist thickening to April rain.

Dixie, my third wife, has sued me for divorce.
Daughter Marilee has dropped out of sight,
somewhere between the Robert Street bridge in St. Paul
and the Boatmen's National Bank of St. Louis.
Son Scott writes from Stateville that prison guards
have taken his poems, his notebook of new songs.

Yes, this empty house has heard angry words too:
"cheat," "bitch," "I'll break your goddamn neck."

Gents, listen to me now and listen to me well.
Some men should always get drunk alone.

CARL YELENICH
One Tough Hombre

I was red-faced, tight-lipped angry
for four, maybe five, whole days.
The truth is, I could have killed someone.
Later, when I started to feel good again,
I knew I was a real son of a bitch.
So I broke a bottle with my fist.
Cuts, lots of blood, some stiffness, some pain.
But it felt so good, so goddamn good.
I only get hurt when I hate myself.
And I'm one tough hombre, my boy.

BEN HILDEBRAND
Father and Son

I can find her gravestone, son,
because I know which one is hers.
I could not forget that.

But there's no one's name on it.
I don't see Great-Grandmother's name.
Who took away her name, Pa ?

Her name's Elizabeth Moss.
Time can be very harsh, my boy.
And the wind never quits.

I'll remember where it's at.
Between the big elm over there
and this gray slab that says Cobb.

Yes, Cobb here and Payne close by.
Hurlbut and Goodenow up the hill.
Proud names, old and proud names.

Did she live her whole life here,
here in Sunflower County, Pa?
Did she see Buffalo Bill?

She was born somewhere in Maine.
The ocean was what she bragged on.
But cornfields have her now.

235

DANIELLE BLUE
Child Abuse

When I spilled tomato juice
on the white living-room rug,
I thought Mama would kill me.
She screamed my name, said
"You awful, sinful child.
Go up to your room
and read your Bible!"
I did what she said,
catching the fire in her eyes,
the raised club of her fist.
I read in *The Song of Solomon:*
"We have a little sister,
and she hath no breasts:
what shall we do for
our sister in the day when
she shall be spoken for?"
And I said to myself:
"I have a little sister, too,
and she has no breasts,
but she's still a young girl yet.
If she never grows them,
then what will she do?
She'll be a nun or an old maid."
And I read in *St. Mark:*
"And John was clothed
with camel's hair, and with
a girdle of a skin about
his loins; and he did eat
locusts and wild honey."
And I said to myself:
"Now that's downright crazy,
a grown man having to wear
those horrible things on him,
and having to eat insects.
I hope I never have to eat
any old bugs for my supper."
And I read in *Ecclesiastes:*
"I returned, and saw under
the sun, that the race is not
to the swift, nor the battle

to the strong, neither
yet bread to the wise,
nor yet riches to men
of understanding, nor yet
favour to men of skill;
but time and chance
happeneth to them all."
And I said to myself:
"I trust this is true,
because I'm not swift or strong,
nor wise or skillful,
and all I want is a chance
to make God want to love me,
even if Mama and Papa
don't love me anymore
and slap and bang these bruises
on my face, on my arms,
on my legs, on my back."

MASON SINCENDIVER
Driving to Town

Mr. Post,
I feel I've been poorly used,
a courtroom Bible
that's to be replaced
but which has never been read.
In my heyday
I was a walking newspaper
and an expert on quitclaims.
An almanac brain
is what I had.
Judge Lord could tell you that.
Say, you're awfully quiet, Mr. Post.
And gloomy too.
But then today
isn't much of a day, is it?
Not with the temperature still
down around zero
and this country road
slick as glass with black ice.
Now, about that position
in the county clerk's office.
Maybe you could,
perhaps, if possible,
put in a word or two
to the right people.
You know those fellows
at the Courthouse,
and they know you.
Sir, you've not heard
a word I've said.
You're not asleep, Mr. Post?
Mr. Post?

WOODY O'NEILL
Outside the Western Auto Store

Calvin wanted to tell his story again
on how he saw the trotter *Speedy Crown*
capture the coveted Hambletonian,
Du Quoin, Illinois, 1971.

Look at that blonde with the big ba-zooms.

Gilbert wanted to educate us,
to let us in on everything he knew
concerning the red-legged grasshopper,
Alfalfa County, Oklahoma, 1954.

Feel 'em, fuck 'em, forget 'em, is what I say.

Bradley wanted to brag and brag and brag
about the bottle cap collection he owned
when he was just a knee-pants kid,
Baltimore, Maryland, 1938.

Now you take your average Arab girl.

Ivan wanted to reminisce a bit,
to explain the important job he once held
at the Ford Hopkins drugstore,
Cedar Rapids, Iowa, 1962.

Anybody know a nice Christian whorehouse?

MILES POTTER
Spooks

On trick or treat night,
the doorbell rang
around seven o'clock.
I opened the front door.
Two little kids stood there.
Their costumes were simple.
Just black masks and white sheets.
"Who is it this time?" my wife said,
her mouth full of glazed doughnut.
"The FBI," I said.
"I forgot to return
my ROTC uniform."
"Ha ha," my daughter said.
"That's a hot one, Pop," my son said.
I gave each kid an apple
and a big popcorn ball.
"Nice getups," I said.
One kid nodded.
The other kid took down
my name and address.

DEREK VREELAND
The Apple Trees of Pioneer Grove

My ring was on her finger
when I took her that day
to the village of Pioneer Grove.
We had a picnic there:
salami, a loaf of bread,
a bottle of French wine.
We walked hand in hand
under the yellow-apple trees,
the fruit round as full moons,
and talked about the poems
of Apollinaire and Villon,
and how to eat a lobster,
and how to sail a sailboat.
"We shall have no secrets
from each other," I told her,
and explained about Esther,
and about Rachel and the children.
"No secrets," she said,
"so I guess you should know
I've been married twice
but divorced just once."
"Damn Pioneer Grove," I said.
"Damn Apollinaire," she said,
and worked my diamond ring
off her ring-worn finger.

SANDRA SIGAFOOSE
Newcomer

This is the first afternoon
since moving to this flat town
I don't sweat with suspicion.

There is no one to talk to,
but the garbage man just asked
could he bum a cigarette.

I am trying now to learn
how to live with tight-lipped folks
who refuse to neighbor me.

TODD LANPHERE
Ice Cream Store

It's a hundred degrees out there,
but thirty degrees cooler in here.
The girl who brings me vanilla ice cream
and coffee in a chipped cup
wears a frayed white apron that blooms
with chocolate and cherry stains.
There's tacky talk from other tables:
"Don't say one word without I tell you."
"Red saw sixteen red-banded leafhoppers."
"Ma's at the farm, canning her wax beans."
"Sure, moths can damage sunflower heads."
"Chicken gravy died when your aunt Chloe died."
I'm a stranger in a strange town.
My dusty car is parked in the dusty street.
I've traveled a long way from Santa Fe.
This western shirt is wet from sweat.
I'd rather not be here, you hear?
A child says to another child,
"Repeat after me, repeat after me:
clothes chest, sugar chest, cedar chest."
A radio back in the kitchen somewhere
plays Chuck Mangione's "Give It All You Got."
I have been, Lord, I have been,
and I'm still eighty-five miles from home,
eighty-five miles from home,
eighty-five miles from home.
The waitress slaps down my check.
I pick my pocket for a tip
and come up with two sticky nickels,
three dull pennies, and a linty cinnamon ball.
Back on Interstate 55 again,
I put plenty of hot, dusty distance
between me and Aunt Chloe's chicken gravy,
moth-eaten sunflower heads, wax beans,
and those red-banded leafhoppers.
Repeat after me, repeat after me:
You're never home till you're home.

243

KIM AUSTIN
Art Class

Be-
cause
there
was
too
much
blue
sky
in
my
real
life
pic-
ture
of
Sun-
flow-
er
Coun-
ty
I
paint-
ed
the
tall-
est
corn-
stalk
there
ev-
er
was
an-
y-
where
an-
y-
place.

LARRY GRAHAM
Empty Beer Can

Bernadette,
my funky blues girl,
you write from Pittsfield
that you don't love me anymore.
Once when we were driving around
the town square
under a big Pike County moon
you threw a beer can
out the window of my pickup.
Tonight, 200 miles away,
it comes bouncing, end over end,
up to my front door.

JIMMY WINGATE
Cob Shed

Across a bare
farmyard that is
home to a duck
and a goose, and
where cornfield trash
blows in from the
harvested fields
of another
good Corn Belt year,
there's a dazzle
of sumac leaves,
and beyond sits
an old cob shed
where inside I
watch my girlfriend
take off her white
cashmere sweater
so two steep hills
of sweet flesh can
come out to play
love games on this
cool after-school
afternoon, and
Helga says she
wants to see my
pecker, she can't
wait all day, so
I say okay
and drop my pants
and pull down my
bulging shorts and
show it to her,
and she says, "Oh
god," and then she
reaches out with
one finger and
touches the tip
of my hard-on,
which is now moist

246

and standing straight
up like a post
office flagpole,
and it hurts me
all over to
watch Helga there,
bare to the waist,
saying, "Don't you
think we better
go back home now?"

AMANDA PURTILL
Four Rows of Sweet Corn

It's strange you should tell me
he's not coming today
to turn the earth in the side yard,
when just an hour or so ago
he said, "I'll be there at ten,
or if not then, then later on,
say, four or five this afternoon."
No, I can't figure him out.
Maybe he's still smarting at something
I said last time he was here,
something about his daydreaming,
gazing off, staring at the blowing trees.
He's touchy, there's no denying that.
He told me the world would keep
whether I grew food or not.
Nevertheless, summer won't be much
of a summer season to me
if I can't watch some squash growing,
and beans and tomatoes,
and my four rows of sweet corn.

RILEY NOVAK
Tables and Chairs

Ho, ho, Jesus, no, I wasn't fired.
Not this time I wasn't, anyhow.
The company failed, went out of business.
Thirty-four years in the furniture game
and they belly up after one bum year.
Oh, life's beautiful, I tell you, damnit.
Nothing like no money and no job
and a credit-card wife and three big kids
eating up everything in the house
that isn't hid or the dog's dinner.
No use ruining my eyesight eyeballing
those useless help wanted ads, neither,
unless I'd take four bucks an hour someplace
no humble high school dropout would take.
Real nice, too, when all you hear all day
is the wife saying over and over,
"Riley, you gotta do something is all."
So I said, "Okay, I'll do something,"
and I drove to the empty factory
and heaved a brick through the front window.
Yeah, I put some sass in that old glass.
The cops came and took me to the station.
They weren't a bit sympathetic, no way.
What do the police know about wage cuts,
layoffs, strikes, lockouts, and shit like that?
Those bastards don't know nothing, nothing.
Ever see a cop house closed down for good?
No, you never, and you never will.

CAMILLE WEBSTER
Bull Durham

You don't hardly never
see that done no more.
The man over there
under the awning
in the ten-gallon hat
and yeller silk shirt
rollin' a cigarette,
not spillin' the tobacco
from a Bull Durham sack,
and lightin' it proud like,
knowin' there's nobody
'round these parts
who can carry that one off,
and watchin' to see
who, if anybody,
has noticed what
an old smoothy cowpoke
just got off the bus
to dazzle all us yokels.
Don't he do that fine?
He sure do.

THAD STEPHENS
"In the Mood"

Dancing to Glenn Miller's "In the Mood,"
"A String of Pearls," "At Last," "Little Brown Jug,"
just the two of us at her house,
the oriental rug rolled up halfway,
playing "In the Mood" over and over,
gliding around slowly, cheek to cheek,
nobody home for hours and hours,
sitting on the couch, a kiss or two,
putting on more Miller, Harry James,
Count Basie, Ellington, Jimmy Dorsey,
the warm, lush sounds of Claude Thornhill's "Snowfall,"
eating cookies, sipping on Cokes,
the time sliding into late evening,
her folks finally coming back,
telling her goodbye, that I'd see her soon,
leaving her a little tearful,
knowing, even at age sixteen,
it would never be this way again.

EMILY DETWEILER
Lyman's Way

Lyman can't tell
the truth at all.
He always makes up
everything he says.
Everything.
I introduced him
to Spider
and Boomer
and Elwyn
and Selwyn.
I said, "This here is
Lyman Lowell."
Lyman said, "Hello.
I come from
Owls Head, Maine,
and I collect
calypso records."
"Owls Head, Maine?"
Spider said.
"Calypso records?"
Boomer said.
"Horse hockey,"
El and Sel said.
They are twins
and often
say the same thing
at the same time.
There was no more talk.
Spider scraped
his shoe on the curb.
Boomer put
his farm cap
on ass backwards.
El and Sel
snorted and sneered
in chorus.
"See you guys," I said.

Lyman and I
left them there
hanging around
on Main Street
and walked across
the train tracks
and went up the street
to my house.
"Lyman," I said,
"you're a fraud."
"I know it," he said,
and he looked
very sad.

VINCENT PEREZ
Sailor

On the poor side of town
the moon shone with a dull glow.
I sniffed coal smoke and exhaust fumes.
I told myself seven times
I didn't have to be there.
Marnie's driveway was fresh gravel.

Strawberry-colored zinnias
flared from a deep-purple vase.
Marnie painted the picture in school.
Now it was framed with care
and hung in the breakfast nook.

"Marnie passed away on her birthday.
Didn't you get my letter?"
Marnie's mother said softly,
her left hand squeezed into a fist.

A car scooted down the street.
Marnie's dog barked at the window.
The house next door went dark.

Marnie's mother poured me a beer.
"How's the navy?" she said.

"I brought Chinese food," I said.

DUANE FORBES
Buffalo Nickel

"In the middle of old red-brick Oak Street
I found a buffalo nickel," I said.

"Mama says to don't track mud in," she said.

"My first favorite coin has always been
the neat-o buffalo nickel," I said.

"Howie squirted me with a hose," she said.

"What I'd like to do from now on is to
round up the buffalo nickel," I said.

"Gracie gave me her gypsy doll," she said.

"I'll bet you among Daddy's army stuff
there's a lost buffalo nickel," I said.

"Look, I'm painting my toenails pink," she said.

"I must see a real live buffalo like
what's on this buffalo nickel," I said.

"You want to touch my navel once?" she said.

"Buffalo nickel, buffalo nickel.
I love my buffalo nickel," I said.

"No one pays attention to me," she said.

RALPH C. KRAMER
Gossip

This is what I heard them say:

"Did you ever get to know Christian Zak?
He liked to settle an argument with a brick.
Almost killed his cousin Elwood
at an Optimist picnic over to Clover Hill."

"Right, Merle Tyner's boy, that's him.
That's the one the youngest Eggleston girl
is going to marry up with next month.
Not a bright kid, but not dumb, neither.
Was in the navy for four years, I think.
Then went deckhand for some towboat outfit,
pushing loads of coal up the Illinois River."

"Lamar Robinson got home late last night
after a billiard tournament downstate
and found the turtle had died.
He can't do it, he can't keep nothing alive."

"Him a lawyer and state senator,
so what does he care for poor people?
He wants big money, crooked or not."

"So he sits back in his wicker chair,
stares for a minute at the orange sun ball
sinking below the ragged cornstalks,
puffs on his Corona Western, and tells me that
twenty-three cents is still the record
for the lowest light bill in this town.
Set by the Chandler sisters in 1919, he says."

"Belle Abercrombie's daughter, Myra,
is unhappy her breasts are so huge.
Lord, you should see her bounce home from school."

"No, I wasn't at Frank's funeral, Clara.
Jane and Cletus didn't go, either,
and they knew him better than I did.
Gracious, even the dead keep a body hopping."

"You all heard me speak of Chester Thigpen.
He fell off his tractor Tuesday week.
When I told Mother about it this a.m.,
I thought she'd never stop laughing.
They found whiskey on him, of course.
You'd think a man in his upper fifties
would learn to control himself a wee bit."

"In 1948, when Truman's campaign train
stopped in Alliance for three minutes,
Pop said, 'The hell with Dewey. I'm for Harry.'
Mom got sore. She thought little Tom was cute."

Yes, that is how they said it.

SCOTT LANSING
Trotters

High in the stands
at our county fair,
I sit beside
an old hunchback
who talks about
Sherwood Anderson,
chomp on a hot dog,
and watch trotters race.
The sulkies rush
down the final
frenzied straightaway.
Cheers curl my ears.
I spill mustard
on my scarlet shirt,
which now looks like
the sunset silks
of the glum driver
who came in last.

ADAM POSEY
Sunday Comics

Look, I don't want to hear about
new storefronts on Main Street,
cracked plaster in the downstairs bathroom,
the Sunflower County Cooperative,
my twenty-fifth class reunion,
what happened to last fall's Indian corn,
Ben's Union Pacific belt buckle,
who just bought a Tiffany lampshade,
when the mortgage payment is due,
Fitzgerald, Hemingway, and Dos Passos,
ten cents off on lemon furniture polish,
why we need to buy a Rototiller,
who wrote "Chattanooga Choo Choo,"
warped bricks at the railroad depot,
the latest Community Chest drive,
tomatoes turning orange on the vine,
ecru lace curtains and chenille bedspreads,
any hymn called "Jesus Paid It All,"
David's Black and Decker workbench,
a polyester doubleknit pantsuit,
why Mr. McCloud won't eat Quaker Oats,
toothpick holders and antique snuff jars,
what high school girl swims nude in the river,
cattails out by Butterfield's pond,
who's got an old limestone fencepost,
Comet, Ajax, or Spic and Span,
the levee at New Orleans, Louisiana,
disgruntled farmers griping about taxes,
Pittsburgh plate glass windows,
three missing packages of Kool-Aid,
the Caterpillar plant in Peoria,
what's the matter with the Chicago Bears,
Fred's poker game at the fire station,
or why Doris Peckenpaugh left town.
I want to hear only one thing:
the Sunday paper smacking the front porch.
I can't wait to learn what's up
with Dick Tracy, Blondie, and Moon Mullins.

259

OTIS K. SIZEMORE
Child in the House

When my son, Sam,
in red heat,
threw his baseball
through the hall window,
I didn't get sore,
for I was already
just as mad as he was
and about ready
to bust up the room,
what with my team,
the Cardinals,
losing 8 to O
to the Phillies
on national TV.
So I grabbed my
Enos Slaughter
Louisville Slugger
and knocked out
two more panes of glass.
"There," I said,
"that's one for me
and one more
for you, my boy!"

FAYE HOCKING
At the Home for Unwed Mothers

Well, for one thing,
I wasn't wearing my stockings that night,
and that's where it got off wrong,
because when he touched me on the knee
I got goose bumps just like that,
and suddenly he was hardly breathing,
and a funny look came into his eyes,
like he had gotten religion real fast
under the spell of a hellfire preacher,
and he pushed me down flat to the car seat
and lifted my skirt and went on from there,
pulling and tugging at my clothes,
and I could say nothing to stop him,
and I wanted him to stop,
and I didn't want him to stop,
and it was like being on a roller coaster,
with my head getting lighter and lighter
and no way to turn back,
and then it was finished,
and he was finished,
and a kind of peace swept through me
and I accepted what had happened,
like when you have a tooth pulled
and you know there's no putting back
what's gone for good,
but I didn't love him more for it,
and I didn't start to hate him, either,
and it's only the calm cuddle of my child
that I'm wanting now,
knowing, and knowing it for sure,
that I'll never get to finish high school,
which was something I wanted too.

LANCE BOOMSMA
Wedding Reception

"Hey, go kiss the bride," I said to my brother Ben.
"I already done that already," Ben said.
"Where is it you're to honeymoon at?" Mother said.
"Galena," my bride said. "Up to Galena."
"You ain't sore she was once your girl?" I said to Ben.
"That's the way life goes," Uncle Ted said.
"Galena?"my sister said. "Why Galena?"
"Cold there this time of year," Aunt Flo said.
"We'll be back in a week," my bride said.
"Better take plenty of sweaters," Mother said.
"We're going via Rockford and Freeport," I said.
"How about that? First class all the way," Ben said.

DAISY COLE
The Housekeeper's Story

The Berry sisters
must always say
the Lord's Prayer
before they go to sleep.
That's one of many firm rules
in the Berry house.
Now Jane Berry kneels,
bows her head,
and says the words
in a clear, sweet voice.
But Janet Berry never kneels,
never does it right at all.
She just jumps into bed,
pulls the covers over her face,
and mumbles like an imp.

"It doesn't make
a damn bit of difference,"
shouts Mr. Berry.
"It does so,"
screams Mrs. Berry.
And they move to the kitchen
to argue about this,
their angry voices rising
above the coffee cups.
Meanwhile, upstairs,
the girls get out flashlights
and cut the heads
off all the photographs
of Mr. and Mrs. Berry
on their wedding day.

BOYD DRAKE
Staying Up Late

A green fly buzzes around the light bulb.
No land to farm, no fun, no road to fame.
Where is that blind girl I knew in Athens?

Ears of corn dream of bin, corncrib, and barn.
There are sweet-running cats in moonlit fields.
Who killed the warm, stained-glass glow of autumn?

Blue flowers decay in this den of books.
Dead vines spell my name on the schoolyard fence.
Should I boil an egg or peel an apple?

One thing is sure: old black funk's got me bad.
My pipe weighs a ton in my smoked-out face.
Why must I feel so damned depressed again?

JANICE NELSON
Community Hospital

"If Kimberly dies,
I'll kill myself," Pa said.
"If Kimberly dies
and you kill yourself,
I'll kill myself," Ma said.
"Please, please, please, please, please
stop that kind of talk at once
or I'll kill both of you,"
Sister Kimberly said,
rising from her pillow,
her face drained of color.
And the doctor came
into the noisy room
and said to Pa and Ma,
"Out, out, out, out, out.
Get out before I kill you."

BRANDON OLDFATHER
Spittoon

It's George Washington's birthday,
a cold, dark, windy night.
Only a few lights burn at the Courthouse.
I walk up past the cannon
and the white-shouldered Union soldier.
My boots squeak in the fresh snow.
The door has been left open.
I go inside and stride down the hall
to where Tara Lindahl works
in the coroner's office.
She clicks off her typewriter.
We shake hands and I give her a big hug.
She knows what I've come for.
"Here it is, it's yours," she says.
"It's the last one we have around here."
I feel like kissing her right on the lips.
This is what I've wanted for some time,
a gen-u-ine brass spittoon.

WARREN EGGLESTON
Nostalgia

I live only in the past, kid.
The present is a flat beer
I poured down the kitchen sink
and the future is a loaded shotgun,
locked in the toolshed
with the busted power mower.
Hooray for Lincoln Zephyrs
and interurban trolley cars.
Three cheers for Jack Armstrong.
The trumpet of Harry James
is sweeter to me now
than it was in high school.
I still carry a smiling picture
of Jeanne Crain in my billfold
and I never miss a single movie
Errol Flynn ever made.
I dream of grammar school fun,
cherry Cokes, Dick Tracy Big-Little books,
and my collection of milk bottle tops.
Bee shit on all that's buzzing around
in this falling down world.
Don't come to me with your news events,
your insane babblings
about men blasting off to the moon
or teenage singers who can't sing.
I just wish I could write
President Roosevelt
and tell him he's doing just fine
and the war is going our way,
and that I got another date
with Marjorie Jo Kincaid
to dance to Tommy Dorsey tonight.
Go get 'em, Cardinals,
beat those damn Yankees.
Touchdown for Frankie Sinkwich!
Oh, there's no doubt about it.
I'm going to stay put
in the fabulous 1940s.
Close the door, children.
Daddy doesn't know you anymore.

KEITH APPLEBEE
Boozing Bigots

Just as the evening whistle blows at the tool plant,
the great western sky blazes up and bleeds to glory.

But men tied to lunch pails are in a mad rush to get drunk.

Did you hear the one about the queer Injun chief and . . .

Forgotten wives slouch in doorways and practice their frowns.
The corned-beef hash burns, the radio blabs on and on.

Well, there was this nigger who hated watermelon and . . .

Any brand of beer will do, any wine, any old hooch.

Yes, sure, I used to be one of these boozing bigots.
Christ, getting smashed was the real business of the day.

268

O. E. MOONEY
Working on the Railroad

Well, here I am in a Rock Island caboose,
eating bread and onions for lunch
and watching a heavy midsummer rain
steam on the Middle Western streets.

"Be good," said Mark Twain,
"and you will be lonesome."

Cold rain in Culpeper County, Virginia.
I was alone and silent there also.

I know how the talk goes, what they say:
"That Mooney, he's no damn fun, you know.
He won't gamble, won't take a drink.
Standoffish, that's what he is."

Why can't I swear, knock a man down?
The railroad is the only body I've bruised.

I need a bad woman to be bad with.
But I'm Mooney, the shy onion eater.

NADINE ORLANDINI
Half a Loaf

The word in McIntyre's meat market
is that McIntyre's wife is dying
and their daughter Jan will get married
six weeks sooner than had been announced.
McIntyre's wife doesn't want to die
until Jan is a bona fide bride.
McIntyre is half happy, half sad.

I bought hamburger and six pork chops
from McIntyre's meat market today.
McIntyre had a smile on his face.
McIntyre had a tear in his eye.
The hamburger was good and tasty.
The pork chops were leathery and tough.
Life, mostly, is half a loaf at best.

IVAN LOOMIS
The Vision

I took *Tess of the D'Urbervilles* with me
to my secret place at the riverbank,
a quiet, willow-shaded spot
where the Ausagaunaskee narrows
and bends away to the southwest.
I swam in the muddy summer water,
then stretched out on the warm grass.
Soon I was asleep, with Tess in my arms.
The sun was sinking fast when I awoke,
and I saw a naked girl
come out of the shimmering river.
She looked fantastic:
dark-brown hair, big-nippled breasts,
small waist, great-muscled thighs,
deep-fleshed buttocks, plump calves,
and a face I would love till death.
Then she moved closer,
there in the sun-dazzled afternoon,
moved slowly, so very slowly,
swinging her wide hips,
her tongue licking her upper lip.
The willow leaves stopped their shaking.
There were no more insect noises
in the mouths of flowering weeds,
no nervous bird chirpings.
Everything was still as God.
I could hardly breathe.
"Tess," I said out loud, at last,
"I'll have to take you home now.
You've got me much too excited,
and Mr. Hardy doesn't know where we are."

FANCY SCARBOROUGH
Osage Orange

The school playground.
No one was playing there.
Saw a ball no kid wanted.
Or some kid forgot.
Took the ball back home.
Never saw a ball like that.
So rough, so strange.
"What game goes with this ball?" I said.
Mom laughed and so did Dad.
Carolyn laughed too.
"That's no ball," Dad said.
"A ball that's not a ball?" I said.
"It's an Osage orange," Mom said.
They all laughed again.
Went outside to play catch.
"It's not a ball," Dad said.
"Here, catch," I said.
Mom caught it, she caught it.
"See, a real ball," I said.
So we played in the yard.
Played until dark.
My new ball played great.
Bumpy, old frog-wart ball.
Funny, laughing, green ball.

JOLENE DOERR
Fat

Not being too smart in school
is not so bad to worry me much.
Being fat is something, though.
The other kids tease me all the time.
Before English, after Math,
during Gym, during lunch hour,
and any time they can get a chance.
I'm so awful sick of that dumb rhyme,
"Fatty, Fatty, four by four,
can't get through the kitchen door."
I don't care what Mom and Dad will say.
I'm not going to any more schools
or sit in another class.
And I've locked my bedroom door
so they will know I mean what I mean.
The pain of fat will not quit.
It's like my life has just stopped.
I don't wish that I was dead
But I do wish I was never born.

TY JARVIS
Talkers

We talked about
hummingbirds, coal,
Tom Paine, peach jam,
visions, earthquakes,
locust trees, darts,
snow, grasshoppers,
Mayo Clinic,
petrified wood,
birthdays, rainbows,
Herbie Hancock,
warts, cashew nuts,
icicles, zoos,
Olympic Games,
haymows, biscuits,
Teamsters Union,
Jamaican rum,
nuns, Ferris wheels,
Sherlock Holmes, floods,
Huguenots, geese,
avocados,
sun, dust, heat, drought,
Winston Churchill,
Korean War,
popcorn balls, owls,
farms, Langston Hughes,
Chicago Bulls,
insomnia,
and then she said,
"Let's talk about
us for a change,"
and I said, "Yes,
let's talk about
us," but there was
nothing to say
or anything
we wanted to
say, I should say,
and we left each
other speechless

274

under the town
water tower
without even
saying, "I'll see
you" or something
like, "Let's meet soon
and talk about
Dylan Thomas,
dew, mist, fog, rain,
angels, eyebrows,
foreign movies,
Stan Kenton, toads,
eggnog, antiques,
honeysuckle,
North Dakota,
crows, lightning rods,
Vincent Van Gogh,
fish tanks, streetcars,
haunted houses,
pea soup, candles,
Wabash River,
rape, Maine coon cats,
patchwork quilts, soap,
tea, alarm clocks,
windmills, trombones,
animal rights,
banana splits,
New Zealand, and
Anton Chekhov."

PHYLLIS NESBIT
  Chinese Restaurant

At our town's Chinese restaurant,
one Chinese-blue neon letter
has just given up the ghost.
MOO CHOW'S now reads MOO COW'S.
Does Moo care? Is he perturbed?
"No," he says. "Moo care only
if folks don't eat chow at Moo Chow's."
"You mean Moo Cow's," I said.
"Chow, cow, plow, sow," he says.
"Moo Chow don't give Shanghai shit."

HOPE GIBBS
Fire and Water

We were down again
on a fishing Sunday
to Kankakee, Illinois,
bitching as usual
about the river
you called filthy.
It has already been
a dozen or more Septembers
since you were there
in that old town,
flat on your back
at Borg's rest home,
Uncle Herbert's picture
on the bedside table.
I heard from the Swede
you were hemorrhaging
when that awful fire
broke out in the kitchen.
They carried you, he said,
from the second floor
and put you under
the white oak tree.
You died there,
smelling the smoke
of burning drapes
and cheap paint,
your last thoughts
turning perhaps
to the clear, cold waters
of a long ago
Canadian childhood.

ROBERT EVERWINE
Son

She's kind of plump,
but, no, she's not pregnant.
And here she comes now,
back from a trip to the store,
hair in her eyes,
a swelling mosquito bite
decorating her forehead.
"Norma," I say to her,
"you're really a sight."
Her chin quivers
and she bites her lower lip.
The bag of groceries
crashes to the kitchen floor.
A can of sockeye salmon
rolls under the table
and smacks against the stove.
She begins to cry.
I kiss her once on the nose
and twice on the mouth,
then we climb the steep stairs
and make love on the bed.
We keep on trying.
Year after year
we keep on trying and trying.
But poor, patient Norma
never gets pregnant.
Look, she just wants a baby.
I want a son!

NATHAN ACKERMAN
In Kreb's Kandy Kitchen

Now don't forget, Lefty, to look me up
when you want those wisdom teeth yanked.
I'm above Western Union in the McFee Block,
and in Yellow Pages my name is number one.
There's no need to hurry, just take your time.

You say you've been in pain now and then?
But it's not a tooth, nothing up there in the head?
What? Your pitching arm is where you hurt?
Coach Claypool blames it on your bum teeth?
You yelp like crazy when you throw the ball?

Maybe it's your teeth, and maybe not, my boy.
I'll check it out, but for right now,
come over to the window and open your mouth.
No, Lefty, first take the jawbreaker out,
and the jelly bean, too, while you're at it.

GRACE RODZINSKY
Cocktail Party

My old pinchpenny husband.

Why did I wear this dreadful dress,
the lizard-green dress with pink lace?

For the main and simple reason
you don't give me any money,
the white dress is out of season,
and I haven't any money.

Hey, I made a rhyme for you,
a little poor-wife rhyme for you,
a rhyme for you, rhyme for you.
Will these small wonders never cease?

But you say you like my hair, my face?
And you'll excuse this dowdy dress?

Oh lucky me. Oh amazing Grace.

CORKY NOLAN
High School Blues

Basketball game. We win. The Cornhuskers win.
Now the parking lot. It snows like crazy here.
I get out the flask for a blast of sauce.
Blonde cheerleader Debbie talking to five boys.
She squeals at the blowing snow stinging her legs,
then scrambles into a midnight-blue Oldsmobile.
The boys scrape the windshield and they drive off,
bright headlights dazzling the fresh snow.

It's no use, there's too much competition,
too many handsome guys around with Hollywood smiles,
with cunning questions and clever answers,
with easy charm and charming ease.

When I get home to Mulberry Street
I give Debbie's box of Valentine's Day candy to my mother,
to whom I've been downright hateful
for three, four, five months.

I'm sorry about my life, about girls.
I keep too many pointed breasts on my brain.

Damn them all. From now on, boy,
it's eyes in books or straight ahead.

But then there's that new brunette in Chemistry,
with calves more curved than sickle moons.

I think very hard on her in bed.
My hand works between my thighs.

PHIL DUDLEY
Cow in the Creek

I run zigzag through apple trees,
then cut across Howard Early's farm
to watch Owl Creek fill up
with water from a summer rainstorm.
Standing in the rushing stream,
beyond the wreckage of a collapsed shed,
is a Jersey cow chewing on a pale flower.
I stare at cow, cow stares back at me.
Cow's eyes are sad and dark as plums.
Cow is wet, and she is thinking
that I'm the ghost of Johnny Appleseed?
or the lost milker of Sunflower County?
or the Lone Ranger?
Or maybe cow is thinking
she's seen me someplace before:
wading in the Kishwaukee?
boating on the Illinois?
fishing in the Fox?

Hush, you birds, quiet down.
Quit that noisy chatter.
For cow is thinking, thinking, thinking,
bamboozled in a swollen creek
full of brown rainwater,
warped boards, an old tire,
and a floating garden of torn flowers.

Go, get on home now, Ernestine.

Eva? Eleanor? Ethel?

LEWIS PERCY
Goodbye

At last.
I've really done it.
Under a star-crazed evening sky,
I have slipped away
in an empty Burlington Northern boxcar,
which is rumbling west
toward the Mississippi River.
And like an old-time vaudeville comedian
playing the tank-town circuit,
I must ham it up:
first with my Charlie Chaplin routine,
then with a few Fred Astaire dance steps.
Now I stand erect,
my right hand over my left breast,
and I swear again to quit for good
my fumbling around
with overdue bills and Saturday night bridge,
with diapers and lawnmowers,
with iron boss and stone wife.
The lavender breath of lilacs
works deep into my lungs.
I swell like a silo in country fog.
A fresh start is what I've got,
a new place to hang a new hat.
I tell you, my friend,
there will be no sad longings for me,
no looking back.
Never.

WYNTON THATCHER
Duets

The girl next door,
with the wild red hair
and Scottish accent,
said she could hear me
play my clarinet
through the open window
of my bedroom,
and although I was no
Buddy DeFranco
or Artie Shaw,
I sounded all right
for a young man
still in junior high school,
but that my tunes
could use some strings,
which would give them class,
so she came to the house
and brought her cello
and we played duets
on the patio,
in the living room,
on the screened front porch
all summer vacation,
through June lawnmowers,
through July firecrackers,
through August barbecues,
and Prairie Street
never heard such strange,
such free-form music
like that again.

BILLY UNDERWOOD
Memorial Day

Uncle gives his Chevy horn three sharp toots.
Mother bangs shut her new reincarnation book
and puts on rubber boots and Father's black raincoat.
The moment has come. There's no way out.

I slump in the back seat and say nothing,
a temporarily benched home run slugger
rubbing spit into the pocket of a catcher's glove.

The car starts and we're off to the graveyard.
Mother clutches two American flags from the dime store
to plant at the foot of Father's headstone.
Uncle drives slowly, tries to stay calm.

Father is only a fading memory these days,
a crabby guy who could throw a neat knuckle ball.
When I dropped a toss his scorn burned like fire.

Mother wouldn't let Father out of her sight.
Father put up with Mother as long as he could,
then left home to join the air corps again.
He crashed in West Berlin. Mother never cried at all.

Uncle pushes the flags into the spongy earth.
Mother raps on Father's carved stone and says,
"You won't get away with this, Howard. I won't let you."

A big grackle flies across the wet pine trees.
Mother's eyes look awful funny, real spooky.
"Let's get out of here," I say to Uncle.
"Mother is hating Father more than ever now."

IRIS EXLEY
Things and Stuff

Too many things are busted here.

Sister Sharon doesn't live here now.
A half-baked breadwinner from Baltimore
took her away to his mansion house.

She was the star queen of this town.
All the boys drooled in hot pursuit.
Ma knocked them off the porch with a broom.

Busted oven, broken snowblower.

Last Saturday afternoon we went
to the new Farm and Fleet store
and saw things and stuff, including
smoke detectors, flashlights,
electric razors, waffle irons,
coffee makers, electric knives,
food processors, stoneware crock pots,
electric can openers, blenders,
tea kettles, electric fry pans,
steak knife sets, microwave cookers,
electric blankets, humidifiers,
clock radios, electric fans,
vacuum cleaners, screwdriver sets,
and lots and lots and lots more stuff.
We rummaged up and down the aisles
and picked up and looked over some
snow shovels, grease guns, toasters,
hair dryers, and space heaters,
and then it was time to go home,
time to get the hell out of there,
and we left with nothing at all
and rattled the Ford back to Tenth Street.

Busted icebox, broken lawnmower.

Sister Sharon has a marriage license,
a mink coat, six red vinyl barstools,
and a *Wall Street Journal* for a husband.

She wears no bra and she needs none.
Her big breasts stick straight out,
firm and sturdy as hardened balls of dough.

Too many things are broken here.

ROWENA STARK
Snowman

I marveled up my snowman one more time.
But no children came.
The postman came.
The soft-water man came.
The gas man came.
They were all very kind.
My snowman lost a lot of weight.
I tried hard to be patient.
The postman left.
The soft-water man said he couldn't stay.
The gas man had to hurry off.
We waited in love's limp weather.
Just me and Charley Snowman.
But no children came.
No bright eyes anywhere.

HERMAN FOX
Happy Hour

"Got time for one more beer and a shot is all," he said.
"Aren't we still going to coon hunt tonight?" I said.
"I don't think so, the missus come back early," he said.
"Let's go straight from here, no need to go home," I said.
"No, can't, the old lady is out in the truck," he said.
"There's a cloud behind each silver lining," I said.
"You mean there's a woman in every cloud," he said.

BARRY MACMILLAN
Cold Front

When he got on my ass about school,
I sassed my father good,
and he, red in the face, knocked
a peanut-butter sandwich out of my hand.
It went flying across the living room,
landing near the bookcase.
"Now pick it up," he said.
"I won't," I said,
and pushed out through the screen door.
"Come back here," he said.
"I won't," I said.
I walked down the street,
glad to get away from him and home.
On my way back for supper
I stopped at the drugstore
and bought my father a White Owl cigar
and put it by his plate.
"You didn't have to do that," he said.
"I know it," I said.
"Then you're sorry you spoke to me
in that tone of voice?" he said.
"No, I'm not," I said.
"You're a hard case," he said.
"So are you," I said.
"Pass the vinegar," my father said.
"Yes, sir," I said.

CLARK SPRINGSTEAD
Fender Sitting

You want to learn, you got to listen:

"There are gospel words burning in my blood."

"I've got me a big snowplow on my truck
and they call me when a blizzard hits."

"Now what do you make of a strong kid
who lies around all day on his bed
writing nothing but work songs?"

"Mom's driving out to South Dakota next week.
I told her to miss the Corn Palace in Mitchell."

"Like his father before him, by God,
Father was one of them hard-sell preachers
which spend all their growed-up years
poaching in the poor fields of piety."

"I have seen that Corn Palace one time.
My, it was a disappointment, let me tell you."

"Will won't get a job, won't look for work,
and drives us all batty in the head
with his humming and banjo strumming."

"Snow's coming middle December,
but this old soldier can deal with it."

"Myself, I'm cool as gentle Jesus."

An education is where you find it.

LISA GENTRY
Last Morning

It was sad
when he was
dying that
last morning,
for he held
Mother's hand
and he looked
into her
crying eyes
and said, "Oh
Elsie, I
love you so,"
and Mother
began to
moan some more
and we felt
terrible
and shook our
heads because
Mother's name
was Dolly,
not Elsie,
and all those
"oh Elsies"
on his lips
were like sharp
blows and I
finally
said, "Okay,
Dad, okay,"
and we knew
who Elsie
was and what
she meant to
him, even
if Mother
never knew
who Elsie
was, and we

kissed him with
a goodbye
tenderness
until the
nurse said, "I'm
sorry, so
sorry" and
told us it
was over
and Dad was
in heaven
now and no
longer in
pain, and I
blew my nose
and looked out
the window
at the snow
coming down.

IRENE KOZAK
Telephone

The telephone rang three times last week.
My, those were gay old times.
There were folks asking to speak to
Frankie Bell,
Pamela Grace McCracken,
and Mrs. Hunnicutt.
They all wanted to talk and talk and talk.
Oh what tales they had to tell me.
"Well, I got to run," they'd say at last.
And I'd say, "Me too."
It's good to chat with anybody who calls,
even if they know I'm not
Frankie Bell,
Pamela Grace McCracken,
or Mrs. Hunnicutt.
I wonder who they think I am?
I wonder who I think I am.

SAM BUCKNER
Lovers' Quarrel

At half-light I gaze at muddy water.
The brooding face of the Ausagaunaskee River
is not the face of a drowned boy
who went wading a little too far
with fishing pole or hunting dog,
nor the face of the drunk from out of town
who fell off the railroad bridge one spring night
after losing at poker, or was it pool?
No, there are no haunting faces here,
no one to remember, no one to grieve for.
But back beyond weeping willow shadows,
a gravel road, and withered catalpa blossoms
is the face of an unhappy country girl,
wet-eyed now over a packed suitcase,
hoping to catch the next bus for Mattoon
so she can tell Mama and Papa
about the mean mouth she got married to.

NORBERT JOYCE
Drummers

Yellow-lit railroad coaches
and new towns at blue dawn
run through my memories.
I had a good territory:
the Dakotas, Wisconsin,
Minnesota, and Iowa.
I kept my sample cases tidy,
was neat and courteous,
and knew my products cold.
Believe me, sonny,
they respected your old grandpa.
What did I sell? you ask.
Medicines was my line:
stuff for headaches, asthma,
stomach troubles, hay fever,
even female complaints.
I knew all the hotels,
the depots, the boardinghouses
from here to Aberdeen.
Drummers were a special breed
back in them long ago days.
"Knights of the grip"
was what they named us,
or "commercial tourists,"
or "trade interviewers."
We were good at pranks,
told many a tall tale,
and were fresh as April dew
with all the country girls.
When the company went broke,
I sold cars in La Crosse,
then worked for Ward's
in Duluth and Des Moines.
But it was a real comedown:
no more good talk with friends,
no more nights in St. Paul,
and no more railroad coaches
with them yellow lights.

What's that again?
What are female complaints?
Well, boy, you see—
I think it's time for bed.

SEAN KANE
At the Eighth-Grade Dancing Class

I danced with May
of the fat butt,
with Sue of the
moist hands, with Kay
of the bad teeth,
with Lou of the
slow feet and then
I went on home
to bed and dreamed
about dancing
with Peg of the
warm smile, with Bess
of the cute nose,
with Meg of the
gold curls, with Tess
of the strong thighs.
"Well, what about
Ingrid of the
big tits?" said my
brother, Jacob.
"Do you have dreams
about dancing
with her?" "No, I
don't," I said. "When
I think about
her I don't think
about dancing."

MARJORIE YORK
Brown

I sweat home brew
in the unforgiving sun.
She takes a last bite
of her sour apple,
throws the core on the dry grass,
and tells me how her life went to pot:
"We got married at eighteen,
two months out of high school.
Niles was a big drinker, even then.
Couldn't, or wouldn't, keep a job.
Was always going off
to fish with his buddies.
But fishing for what?
There were no fish.
Women was what they were after.
He wasn't fooling me a bit.
When he hit that bridge,
driving drunk in his pickup,
I didn't cry.
I'd already done plenty of that."
She's a new widow
and I'm an old widow.
Her sob story is much like mine,
but I say nothing
and let the woman writhe on the rack
of marital complaints.
"Niles never left money enough
to bury the corpse,
may God grind his bones," she says.
Cicadas scream in the elm trees.
I watch the apple core turn brown
in the unforgiving sun
and sweat home brew.

ESTELLE ETHEREGE
Seventy-Five

Thursday I'll be seventy-five years old.

Coming up the hill from the dry goods store,
I can see that my house is in sad shape.
The front porch sags, a bay window is cracked,
and the garden is full of brittle weeds.

Inside, the grape drapes are faded and worn,
the icebox mumbles Portuguese or French,
the canary won't sing, the dog is deaf,
and my bed is held together with twine.

Estelle, the evening breeze is turning cold.

WILBURN MILLER
Bud

In grade school
the teachers
they always called me
Wilburn,
and as I look back
to them days,
that could have been
the reason
right there
why I hated the place
so awful much,
why I knifed up
every desk I sat behind
and wouldn't never
say a single word
to nobody,
or read from a book,
or put numbers
on the old blackboard,
because my name
is Bud,
Bud is my only name,
just Bud,
and no one
in the poolroom
or on the section gang
dares to call me
Wilburn,
because they know
damn well
I would swear
something terrible
and scratch and bite,
so does this
keep me out
of the army,
doctor?

HEIDI KOENIG
Slow Day at the Office

The raindrop
on the right
would have
overtaken
the raindrop
on the left
in the match race
down my
windowpane
but
the raindrop
on the right
ran smack into
the blood bug
of the week
so
the raindrop
on the left
won
easily
and that' s
when
the big boss said
"Heidi!"

SELMA SKOGLAND
Peanut Butter

When Marty came home from the marines,
after getting a dishonorable discharge,
he lost no time in telling us
that he was going away to become a hairdresser.
Dad merely shrugged, grunted twice,
and went right on reading the night ball scores.

Then Jack joined the Salvation Army
and wrote that he was content for once,
working up a righteous sweat on a bass drum
and saving souls on street corners.
Dad didn't even grunt this time.
He only coughed and blew his nose.

But no goofy sons were about to outdo Dad.
When it came to being nuts, he was the whole tree.
In fact, just yesterday he took off for Mexico,
taking the family's red Edsel,
eleven jars of Peter Pan peanut butter,
and the plumber's teenage wife.

DOUG CHANDLER
  Television

I have decided, Doris,
that it's time to stand up tall
and let you have it flat out.
Until you get yourself a TV set,
I'll not sit any more nights
on your electric-blue rayon plush couch.
Do you understand, Doris?
I'm missing too many exciting shows,
too many athletic thrills.
Also, the act we put on
night after night after night
will never be a big hit.

GUY HANSEN
Retirement

I quit my stool at the Spot-Lite Diner,
a toothpick jumping between my teeth,
then moving over to the steamy window
I watch the long, quiet rain.

Standing here, cracked hands unclosing, closing,
wearing a blue sweat-faded work shirt,
my laboring man's body grows tense, twitches,
the noon factory whistle blowing shrilly.

I think: *So this is retirement, this empty nothing?*
And feeling cheated, the angry thoughts come:
no wife, no children, no more work to do,
forty years a millwright now drained away.

I step out into Sixth Street muttering to myself,
not noticing the cold, persistent rainsoak,
fears of uselessness and numbing boredom
screaming along the assembly line of my brain.

Turning to duck under a sheltered doorway
to relight a Marsh Wheeling cigar,
my throat is dry as sawdust,
the match flaring, burning down, winking out.

AMY GOGARTY
Dimples

Through the messy
medium of paint,
my daughter makes a green father
and a red mother
on the butcher's paper
I let her have
to watercolor on.
Now who in the world told her
at the tender age of three
that she has Irish on one side
of the family
and Iroquois on the other?
No one, no one at all,
though someday soon she'll know it
and be mighty proud.
Ah, but who's ready
to break the news as to where
those dimples came from?
Now that's another story
and she'll never be too old
to puzzle that.

LUANNE ELLIOTT
Escaping the Holy Rollers

The wind smelled of wet leather.
I wanted summer rain to gallop me down
in a field of flowering weeds.

A squall line was building up in the west.
I heard hooves pound beyond the sun,
drumming across the long flanks of sky.

Two lathered men had come to the house,
burdened with booklets about Jesus.
When they knocked, I could not answer.

Instead, I ran to that high place
in back of the town water tower,
desperate for space and fresh air.

Lightning came and thunder came,
but no rain followed the saddled wind.
I remained dry as Noah's ark.

Later on I pulled up carrots
by the light of an oat-straw moon,
then slept, dreaming of wild-eyed horses.

TROY BOWMAN
Forgiven

I drove away mad
under a hard hat of curses,
accusations, and hate.
Now I'm on my way back home
to be forgiven again.
A real blizzard is brewing.
Heavy snow begins to drift
across this interstate highway
and make little snow houses.
I sit behind the wheel
of my old Oldsmobile,
turning the radio on,
turning the radio off,
turning the radio on,
turning the radio off,
turning the radio on,
turning the radio off.
She cried when I called her.
"I want to see you," I said.
"Come home," she said. "Come home."
Yes, I've done this before.
And I'll do it again.
The highway is empty and white
and terribly cold.

EDWARD FINLEY
Don't Stop the Carnival

I passed a kidney stone
on April Fools' Day evening.
The pain almost drove me crazy.
Then, ten days later,
I was in a minor car accident
and had to have two teeth pulled,
my mouth no longer a model
of frantic dental care.
Last fall I had a bout with gout.
My sister writes from Fort Worth
that the Finley medical history
also contains lumbago,
asthma, bronchitis, and night cramps.
This noon, home from the hospital again,
after my liver laid me low,
I drove up my sun-dusted street.
My daughter and her friend
were having a tea party on the lawn,
until a squabble broke out
as to who had the cutest doll.
My son came from the schoolyard
where he fell on his head
while trying to hang by his knees
from the chinning bar.
He sobbed and I hugged him.
Just a scare and a headache.
In the kitchen, my wife
was singing to the radio
and burned the corn muffins
she was going to serve with the chili.
I hope they realize
that none of this matters much,
that it's good to be alive,
part of the fumbling family of man.
Here's to the living.
Don't stop the carnival!

WENDELL MAGEE
Second Shift at the Printing Plant

I was the new man on the job, lucky to find work in the land of the minimum wage. After I was there for a few days, my birthday came around and my supervisor, a good-looking woman in her late twenties or early thirties, brought over a birthday card, courtesy of the company. "I'm fifty-nine today," I said. "Oh, come now. Fifty-nine? You're not fifty-nine years old," she said, and gave me a little smile. Jogging and my new grapefruit diet have really paid off, I thought. Damn right I don't look any fifty-nine. More like forty-nine. "How old do you think I am if you don't think I'm fifty-nine?" I said. She took a few steps backward and looked me over the way you'd look over a used car. She could have been Miss February on a machine-shop calendar, standing there in her flimsy blouse and tight-fitting jeans. "Oh, I'd say--I'd say probably fifty-eight," she said. I shook my head, sadly. I felt like some poor son-of-a-bitch who just got pulled over for speeding. "I can't see there's much difference between fifty-nine and fifty-eight," I said. "Yeah," she said, "they are kinda close at that." "Close?" I said. "They're Siamese twins." "Yeah, like welded," she said, and locked her fingers together. We shared a short laugh and I went back to work.

GENEVIEVE SNYDER
Vacationland

Way up in Michigan,
among the loons and loonies
of vacationland,
our last morning by the lake
was filled with fighting.
I mean screaming, kicking,
hair pulling, face slapping.
There was nothing to do.
We were tired of the beach
and bored with the boat.

One more year at Cedar Lodge,
where one week seems like six.
The same ping-pong table.
The same shuffleboard game.
The same dumb magazines.
Only thing that was new
was a huge wasp nest,
cut out of a tree or bush
and propped up in the corner
next to the telephone booth.

But when Mom and Dad got back
from town with the car,
all gassed and oiled up
for the long trip home to
Alliance, Illinois,
we girls posed like angels
in our dry bathing suits,
squinting into August sun,
while Dad aimed his Kodak
and we all said "cheese."

311

ARCHIE HAMILTON
Tale of the Tub

I refused to
answer the phone
and the doorbell.
I was in the
tub reading *Who
Lost an Amer-
ican?* by Nel-
son Algren and
sucking on a
Lowenbrau, and
I was so warm
and comforta-
ble that I said,
"Let them ring and
ring and ring. I'm
not answering."
Algren was so
entertaining
and funny that
I stayed put in
the tub for at
least an hour and
came out with my
nerves all calmed down.
It was a love-
ly evening and
I got dressed and
put on my old
college letter
sweater and my
two-toned venti-
lated shoes and
made myself a
big tossed salad.
I forgot all
about the poor
day at the store
and the unkind

312

remarks that As-
trid overheard
the boss make at
the pop machine
about me, and
I went to look
closely at my-
self in the hall
mirror and said,
"Jesus, man, you're
still a handsome
dude and why aren't
you out on the
town eyeballing
all those female
bowlers at the
Sunset Bowling
Lanes or the chicks
bending over
banana splits
at the drive-in?"

FERN DYSART
Ninety-Two in the Shade

It's a hot summer day.
We are walking slowly, slowly downtown.
We need some cold, cold, cold drinks.
"Why do you always sing 'Fools Rush In'
when you're happy and crazy
and loaded with love?" she says.
The sidewalk sprouts a crop of kids
and toy wheels that puff up the dust.
"Where would an angel fear to tread?" she says.
The bank sign says it's 92 degrees.
That's why we're not rushing no place fast.
Let these sweaty kids flirt with sunstroke.
"So hot, hot, hot," she says.
"Corn growing weather," I tell her,
using the old cliché.

MACK SCARCE
Going Steady

A mad, moon-soaked, May midnight.
I'm walking home past darkened houses.

This wormy shortcut through tall weeds.
My skin is damp with passion sweat.

Pale gold flesh of her plump thighs.
The brown curly hair of her sex.

She tickles, she squeezes, she fondles.
She drives me crazy with kisses.

Think: marry her? or not marry her?
Wild plum drops a white blossom.

Tall brick chimney at Franklin School.
It sticks up like a proud penis.

RUTH ULRICH
Baby

Baby lost no time
in getting bad sick.
I said, "You too, huh?
Are you going to die too?"
I had lost two babies
soon after they were born.
Hardly cleaned up they were.
Doctor told me,
"This baby's okay,
so quit fraying your nerves."
But he wouldn't sleep.
Was mad all the time.
After I breast-fed him,
he would throw up all over me,
then cry and cry.
"He's going to die.
I know it," I said.
Doctor shook me
like you'd shake a raggedy doll.
"Listen here," he said.
"Baby's not going to die."
He was right, of course.
My baby is a big boy now.
Walks the dog, mows the lawn.
When I get the jimjams,
start climbing the walls
about things like warts
or varicose veins,
he pulls on my ear
until I calm down.
"Don't be a baby," he says.
"Don't be a baby."

VELMA WITHERSPOON
Mischief

"It's raining, so what's there to do?"
When my brother says that,
you'd better watch out, that's for sure.
He gets that devilish look in his eyes,
and you can't laugh him into temperance
or calm him with milk and cookies.
When he's bored he turns into big trouble.
He's not the same person at all,
any more than Clark Kent is
after he changes clothes in a phone booth.
We've been through things, Mother and I.
We've been through ink, paint, nails,
floor polish, gasoline, and tar.
And thank the good Lord that Father
has locked up Al's BB gun.
Don't worry, we'll keep our eyes on him
this rainy April afternoon.
Even our dog Pinky is wide awake.
She never has gotten over the shock
of being the first green poodle in town.

BARNEY PRINGLE
Heat Wave

The house smells like we had smelly socks for supper.
Under my chair is no place for your roller skates.
Are you nuts? The Illinois State Fair in this heat?
I sure wish those cicadas would shut the hell up.
Movies, movies, movies, that's all you care about.
No, I ain't worried, a tornado would improve Elm Street.
My front name? Now what kind of dumb lingo is that?
Let your mother explain "opera house." She's old enough.
Go join the 4-H Club. It sure won't bother me none.
Don't call me a grouch, young lady, and I mean it.
What? You drinking another can of Green River again?
I'll sit here and sweat in my shorts if I want to.
Trouble is, anymore, I need a trip away from here.
Monday night and I feel already I've worked a week.

OWEN HENDERSON
Bad Night on Blue Hollow Road

What happened was
was that I blew a left front tire last night
way out on Blue Hollow Road,
about a half mile or so off Illinois 64,
and I'm getting out the tools
and looking around for the Eveready lantern
when a load of doped-up kids pull up
and start to make fun of my trouble.

What happened was
was that they all pile out of the car,
six or maybe even eight of them there were,
including this one puny bit of a girl
taking little noisy sips from a can of beer,
and they commence to push and shove each other,
wanting to work the jack,
and then the tall guy hurts his hand.

What happened was
was that the fat guy gets sore at the girl,
saying she was showing me her underwear,
and the guy with the bad limp
works me over with an ugly brown bottle,
and laying there in the weedy ditch,
I hear them drive off, yelling and cursing,
the road dust drifting across my bloody face.

KELSEY JUDD
Murder

Evenings, when the heat of the day is past,
an eerie orange light burns on the porch
and people stroll by and say,
"That's where it happened, that's the place.
She's dead, she's dead and gone,
and the kids are in the orphanage
asking when their ma is coming back."
Everyone in town knows about it now,
that some crazy man stabbed her six times,
after locking both little girls in the bedroom.
Everyone knows that the cops
are soon to solve the crime.
Everyone knows that for a fact, all right.
But this is what they don't know:
that I picked her up outside a roadside bar
and drove her home for drinks and kisses,
just four weeks ago tonight.
Everyone knows the house is up for sale
and her car was sold for junk.
But only I know about the green shorts
I stripped off her slender body
and stashed inside my shirt.
Though I've tried awfully hard of late
to be nice and natural with folks,
it seems I can't get along with anyone anymore.
What I am is a right shoe on a left foot,
a flat tire on a mountain road,
the last match in a howling wind.
I sit by the cat thinking about that
and wait for the knock on my kitchen door.

CONNIE CARPENTER
Gold

At country dusk,
when sun burns red
and air turns cold,
the lusty wind
plays in fat fields,
rustles long leaves,
crackles dry husks,
and all my days
and all my nights
are ripe with love,
with dreams of corn,
with harvest gold.

With harvest gold,
with dreams of corn,
I'm ripe with love,
and all my nights
and all my days
crackle dry husks,
rustle long leaves,
play in fat fields,
and lusty wind
turns fall air cold,
while sun burns red
at country dusk.

RUBY KIMBLE
Homecoming Game

My poor sister Patsy
had a fly go in her mouth
when she was singing
"The Star-Spangled Banner"
at the homecoming game
over to Champaign.
No, it didn't come out.
She must of swallowed it.
She said it flew in after
she went past the words,
"what so proudly we hailed,"
or some such like that.
She kept her mouth shut
for the entire game.
Didn't even cheer when
Illinois scored a touchdown.
No, I don't know who won.
Buy yourself a paper.

DONALD GUEST
Boredom

She hardly ever leaves the house anymore,
what with cooking the meals,
washing the clothes, scrubbing the floors.
But during the past year or so
she's enjoyed some real good-time afternoons
over at the Congregational church,
gabbing and giggling with the Gaston sisters
and gluing covers back on hymnbooks.

She says I'm bored because I'm boring.
I say I'm bored because she's boring.

She hates my left-wing politics, my goatee,
my choice collection of Japanese prints.

What she does like is cream style corn
and bowling on television.

Listen here, funny Florence has had her fun.
Now, by god, I want mine.

BEVERLY LOMAX
Shipping Clerk

Carelessly cut my
ring finger
while packing
electric fans.
Kept on working.
Kept on packing.
Kept on sucking
blood off my finger.
But blood dripped
on the packages.
Yes, it drip-dropped
on the packages.
Shipped my blood to
Rhode Island,
South Carolina,
and Wyoming.
Didn't pay any mind
to the blood
I was losing.
Then my boss,
a tidy lady,
brought me a bandage
and so my blood,
my summer blood,
was not sent to
Pennsylvania,
Alabama,
or Nebraska.
No, my blood
stayed where it was.
The room was hot,
very stuffy.
I labored on,
shipping fans to
dripping people.
Made it to
coffee break
and drank a can
of Grape Crush

with lucky Louise
who, unlike me,
has a ring
on her ring finger.
It's a diamond,
a little diamond.
I'd gladly bleed
my heart's blood
if it were mine.

LINDA FULGHAM
Ida May and Ida May Not

There's a man sitting on an orange bench
my aunt Ida would sure like to meet.
She's been painting all day and all night.
She put him on that orange bench, you see.
In Ida's painting of man and bench,
the man sits closer to Auntie than
she knows he would if he had a choice.
Yet she has painted herself right there,
kneeling in the sparse grass at his feet.
She is going crazy painting men,
needing men, wanting men she can't have.
It's just too bad the way things go wrong.
Nobody seems to know what to do.
The funny farm is waiting close by.
Will Aunt Ida make it through the night?
Well, Ida may and Ida may not.

JENNIFER PARSONS
Lemonade

We forgot ball and spade
and didn't roller skate
but started a trade
with Karl and Kate
to sell cold lemonade
by the driveway gate
under elm shade.

We labored long and late
and had it made
for it was fine fate
to peddle lemonade
with Karl and Kate
and watch our summer fade
at a three-penny rate.

AUDREY SMITH
  Opinion

With much girlish glee,
my grandmother holds
up her paper fan
and says, "My, it's so
pretty and it still
looks like new and I've
had it for fifty
years." And I say, "Of
course it's pretty and
still looks like new and
you've kept it for all
these years because it
was made in China,
not in Chinatown,
and we should all be
very grateful that
Chrysler just makes cars
and the stereo
and the camera
were made in Japan."
Look, I'm not happy
about the junk this
country makes now, but
that's the way it is.

RYAN HILL
Neighborhood

On the first warm
day of spring, we
jump out of our
beds in a quick
sweat and put on
almost no clothes
and walk barefoot
on the thick grass
and search the trees,
and the sidewalks,
and the blue sky
for our ancient
and famous names,
and if there is
someone new in
the neighborhood
who looks lonely
and needs a friend,
someone from Maine
or just moved from
Mississippi,
I say, "Hello,
my name's Catfish,
the blonde girl here
is Popsickle,
and that little
kid squinting at
the barbecued
sun is called Worms."

JULIE MARSHALL
  In Therapy

Tuesday
I was
saying
to my
mother
I was
sort of
happy
because
I was
sure I
did not
want to
leave the
things of
my world
and the
people
I love
and was
very
sorry
I said
I did
but now
it is
Friday
and I'm
not sure
again.

BRADFORD TULLEY
Lonesome

Lonely? No, not lonely.
Lonesome! Lonesome, as in
"look down that lonesome road."
I'm a Corn Belt farmer's son,
in case you have forgotten that.
Here in the Middle West,
one can grow very lonesome,
which goes beyond just plain lonely.
Lonesome! Do you hear me?
And today I was gosh-awful lonesome,
looking at the bare trees,
the bleak houses, the bland barns,
the oh so empty fields.
You aren't around anymore
to take a little piece of the lonesome
out of my old December.
I'll bet you're not sorry, either.
You don't know what lonely is,
let alone lonesome.
Now that you're in the big city,
you probably don't care a bit
for the boy you left behind
on a corn and cow farm
in cold-lonesome Sunflower County.
Darn you, Caroline,
you won't even write.

MAYNARD LEWIS
Kafka

I stuck out my hand
to shake his hand.
"Better not," he said.
"Got paint on my fingers."
I shook anyway.
"Blue paint," I said.
"What you painting?"
"Daughter's bedroom," he said.
"Ah, a blue daughter,
a morning-glory girl," I said.
"Yes, yes," he said.
"Can I help you?"
I told the man I came
to pick up his wife's copy
of Kafka's *The Castle*
she said she'd loan me.
"This must be it,
here on the table," he said,
and handed me the book.
"You like this stuff?"
"Sure do," I said.
"Franz and I go way back.
We have lots in common, you see.
He had a blue head.
I have a blue hand."
He pulled his ear.
He messed up his hair.
He scratched his stomach.
"I don't get you," he said.
"Goodbye," I said.

PETER VOSBURGH
Return to River Street

That's the place, 12 River Street, our old house,
and your tire is still hanging from the maple tree.
Let's get out of the car, shall we, son?
We'll stand on the sidewalk and have us a look.
Your mother would go right up and ring the bell,
but I don't want to bother them for an inside tour.
Up there where the shades are pulled was your room.
Do you remember the Lionel train you played with?
The track went all around, even under your bed.
I can't believe we've been gone for five years.
Kansas City is okay and the job is going fine,
though you're not as happy as I'd have you, my boy.
You were a real Tom Sawyer or Huck Finn here,
the Ausagaunaskee RIver being just down the bank.
Maybe it was wrong to move, to leave this town.
Some men can be led astray and not even know it.
You'd better not swing on the tire, son.
Come on, get off, it's not yours to fool with now.
Oh, well, go ahead and have yourself some fun,
then let's get a cold pop and get back on the road.

STEPHANIE MORAN
Sad

I
feel
so
sad
a-
bout
the
leaves
they
can 't
fly
south
for
the
win-
ter.

ELLIS BUTTERFIELD
Leaning Barn

When the wind starts to blow hard
I go out to take a look,
because I said Amos Swan's
red barn would collapse before June
and Amos said it would not,
and I said it surely would,
and he said it surely would not,
and I said it would, it would.

So we two left it that way,
not going on and on with
our alternate "woulds" and "would nots,"
but let me put it like this:
that doomed old barn leans more east
with every passing day,
and one big kicking-ass wind
will prove me right and Amos wrong.

My wife, Ann, says I'm a child,
but I say Amos is the child,
and she says I always have
to be right, no matter what,
and I say she's got it wrong,
it's Amos who's got to be right,
and this time he's the one who
will eat some crow pie, not me.

HOLLY JO ANDERSON
Bein' Poor

We live in a too confinin' trailer
with two busted clocks,
a cracked mirror, and no maw.

Our paw is out of work agin.
He has a little drinkin' problem
and his ears don't match.

Flodeen greets all trains,
all Greyhound buses,
and winks at good lookin' strangers.

DeWayne draws naked ladies,
fools with mice and matches,
and picks scabs at church meetin'.

Me? Oh, I do what I can do:
darnin' socks, stealin' fruit,
helpin' Paw get his clothes off.

We don't like it bein' poor.
But things they start out bad
and they just stay bad.

Last year we was in Taylorville.
This year it's Alliance.
Nobody's tellin' 'bout next year.

TOOKIE THORNHILL
Cleaning Up the Yard

We had a loud windstorm most of last night.
It was hard for me and Teddy to sleep.
Mom said she didn't get a single wink.
We all went outside and looked at branches.
The wind broke branches off every tree.
"Well, there's our firewood for next fall," Mom said.
Daddy and Teddy they just shook their heads.
"We got heaps of hard work to do," I said.
"You best stay away, Tookie," Teddy said.
Daddy got out his saw with the sharp teeth.
"I'll do the sawing," he said to Teddy.
I made a pile of the hugeous huge leaves.
I carried seventeen leaves to the curb.
Teddy said I wasn't helping any.
Daddy said I was too helping any.
There were leaves, leaves, leaves all over the grass.
It took me tons of ages to pile them.
Daddy sawed those big branches up real good.
"Let me saw for awhile now," Teddy said.
Daddy said no and brushed Teddy away.
My work began when my fun was not fun.
It was tempting to quit and play with dolls.
But I wanted to piss with the big dogs.
That's something I heard Daddy say one time.
He said it to Mr. Willis next door.
Mom doesn't like that kind of talk one bit.
Piss is one naughty word she won't stand for.
Daddy made dozens of little branches.
"Okay, let's stack these nice and neat," he said.
"If I can't saw, I won't work," Teddy said.
"Tookie, you come help me, then," Daddy said.
"Piss," I said to Daddy, "piss, piss, piss, piss,"
and then I ran down the street with Teddy.

337

ELLEN OPDYCKE
Husband

The one-legged house painter,
my dearly beloved husband,
stands on the topmost rung
of a tall ladder that leans
against the whitest house
in Alliance, Illinois.
His cap, torn at the crown,
is spattered with brown paint
from the big job he performed
on Truck Catingub's horse barn.
But his coveralls are clean
and a new red bandanna
hangs like a bright flag
out of the right rear pocket
where he squirrels his change.

The one-legged house painter
has been on that ladder
painting the same colonial house
for more than seventeen years now.
Through my kitchen window
I see him there every day.
Never mind the banker's wife
who fainted when he fell
and the screaming ambulance
that took him away to die.
Forget that the old mansion
was torn down last week.
And ignore, if you please,
that his favorite brush
is as hard as Rover's bone.

338

GERALD WAGNER
Student

When she unhooks
her brassiere and
the soft fruit of
her breasts glow in
the lampshine, we
take our first-time
lovemaking up
to her bedroom.
And when I tell
her I love her,
even though I
don't think I do,
she shuts her eyes,
grinds her big teeth,
and says, "Gerald,
take off your shoes
and socks, put your
pants and shirt on
that straight-back chair,
don't park your gum
on the bedpost,
watch those knees now,
kiss me first." Oh,
boy, it's very
plain that nothing
will ever change.
I will always
be her student
and she will be
forever Miss
Axelrod the
English teacher.

MURRAY HARRIS
Fall of 1956

I wore my Stevenson button
and walked the seven blocks to downtown.
A damp wind blew some brown leaves
across the warped bricks of the sidewalk.
The girls from the Farmers National Bank
met the girls from the department store,
and over white-bread sandwiches
at Swindell's soda fountain,
jabbered about new jobs and old boyfriends.
Then the talk turned to politics.
"Adlai's too intellectual for me,"
said the middle-aged stenographer,
displaying fried-egg earrings.
"I can't follow him at all,"
said this waitress with Maybelline eyes.
"I'm not going to vote again
until they get some candidates with hair,"
said a blonde, and hee-hawed into her milk.
I finished my lemon phosphate,
lit a Pall Mall cigarette,
then spun off my hard wooden stool
and went out into the nippy air.
I meandered halfway around the Square.
McCutcheon's men's store window
featured a mannequin wearing
a winter-heavy plaid shirt.
At the magazine and card shop
I picked up the latest *New York Times*
and bumped into Toby from the toy store.
We talked about the maple trees
that flamed on the Courthouse lawn,
the winless high school football team,
and the presidential election.
"Stevenson doesn't stand a chance," he said.
"Eisenhower has done a bum job," I said.
"Nothing but blunders abroad
plus confusion and chaos at home."
"General Ike still gets my vote," he said.
"I suppose we'll get a film star next,

some boob from Hollywood," I said.
"Let's get serious," he said.
"You don't think it can happen?" I said.
"No, I don't think it can happen," he said.
"He'll be a Republican, too.
You can bet on that," I said.
Toby glanced at his Mickey Mouse watch.
"Got to get back to the toys," he said.
"Got to buy a warm shirt," I said,
and I did and walked home depressed
in a cold rain that lasted all day.

EILEEN CHRISTENSEN
Class Reunion

Say, I've
never
recog-
nized so
many
people
I've nev-
er seen
before.

Hey, it's
real good
to see
you, Jan,
I mean
Joan, no,
sorry,
forgive
me, Sue?

LAMAR WOCKENFUSS
Friendly Persuasion

The damp corn silk
sticking out
of this ear of sweet corn
is the pubic hair
of my blonde girlfriend,
who just asked,
while running her hand
under my gold shorts,
if we could go
to the movies tonight
and did I have
enough money
for hot buttered popcorn?

JASON FOSTER
Impotence

Frosty
wind blows
through my
groin and
love sweat
grows cold
on your
bare thighs.

Well, no
wonder,
sweetheart,
it's that
old man
winter
come round
again.

IRMA GILLESPIE
Chicken Bone

This morning I found a chicken bone
under my bed, if you can beat that.
The orange cat got in the garbage again.
No wonder I dreamed of you and me,
hand in hand, oh so lovey-dovey,
at the annual Elks picnic.
That was summer of 1964.
Then before you could blink your blue eyes
we're looking at 1965,
and when the next picnic came around,
you were there, but with someone else.
I watched you win the three-legged race,
wishing it were our legs tied together.
Damn cat, dragging picnic-love dreams
into my dreaming, single-bed room.
And damn you, Danny, for coming back,
if only in a silly dream of mine.
After you left the county for keeps,
I thought I had you junked for good,
dropped in a bag with other scraps
and put out on the Monday curb
for the garbage truck to haul away.
Of course when you were living here
you knew I had a crush on you.
In September 1963,
you said, obviously amused,
"Who is that strange girl behind the oak tree?
She follows me wherever I go."

WESLEY HARKNESS
Why He Didn't Repair the Bookcase

I tried.
Right after school.
I couldn't do it.
The wood splits.
Damn nails.
Guess they're just too big.
Or I'm clumsy.
I tried.
Here's your hammer.
It hits pretty good.
Damn nails.
Hate antiques.
Nothing but old junk.
Do it yourself.
I tried.

VON BIGELOW
Screwdrivers

Don't say you don't remember.
You're the girl who told me
her fantasy was to be
a construction worker.
It was at Tony Paulson's house
in Mason City, Iowa.
We sat out under the pear tree
and sipped our screwdrivers
and watched the evening's fireflies
turn on their magic light-show.
You laughed loudly when I said,
"Look at that poor old porch.
It could sure use some strong nails
in some important places."
"I'll get my hammer," you said.
The party droned on inside.
Lots of subdued conversation.
Someone was pounding the keys
of the baby grand piano,
demolishing one of those
turn-of-the-century tunes.
You told me you graduated
from Colorado State
and were now very depressed,
didn't know what to do next.
I said I knew what to do next
and kissed you on the lips.
"Do what you feel like doing.
It's the only way," I said.
"Dare to fail, right?" you said.
"Yes, dare to fail," I said.
We were getting to be friends
and getting pretty friendly, too.
Don't say you don't remember.

SIDNEY LANE
  Friend to Friend

I have always
been impressed
with you tough guys
who do stuff
I won't do,
or can't do,
or would be afraid
to try to do.
If you remember,
I said "hooray"
when you rafted
the Colorado,
"way to go"
when you climbed
that suicide peak
out in Washington,
"marvelous"
when you hunted
wild boar with
bow and arrow
down in Georgia.
But listen up,
old buddy boy,
I got to tell
you something now.
If you parachute
out of that
death-trap airplane
one more time,
we aren't going
to be friends
too much longer.
Look, man, every time
you daredevil
another triumph
I feel smaller
and smaller.
You don't know
what it's like
to bob through life

348

without some balls.
One of these days
I'm going to
go away someplace
and hide among
the little people
of this earth,
my smallness
melting between
my meager legs.

GORDON DALRYMPLE
Having Fun with Dick and Jane

"Do you want to go with us
to the flea market?" she said.
"I could never figure out
why anyone would want those things
around the house," I said.
"What things around the house?" he said.
"Now what kind of folks
go out and buy fleas?" I said.
"Are you nuts or something?" she said.
"I don't keep fleas," I said.
"You're putting us on, aren't you?" he said.
"Cats, parrots, dogs, rabbits,
hamsters, ants, goldfish are okay.
But thumbs down on fleas," I said.
"Yes, you're crazy," she said.
"Maybe snakes or turtles
or some white mice, but no fleas.
Fleas is going too far," I said.

LLOYD KELLOGG

The Man Who Played Clarinet in the High School Band Back in 1936, But Then Never Amounted to Anything Much After That, Is Here Again Today, Folks

I'm rooted to this curbstone.
I won't vamoose, won't leave from here,
though my soaked shoes grow sloppy
and my shirt sticks like a stamp.
The Fourth of July. American flags.
It's a parade is what I'm waiting on.
Hey, look there, here it comes now!
My old excitement is coming too,
because right down Illinois Street
the band, the high school band,
with blare of brass, crash of drums,
is stepping off smartly in the rain.
There I am. That's me. Right there.
See my snazzy clarinet?
Yes, sir, I'm a real proud one today.
I'm really strutting my stuff
before two dozen relatives
just in from Jericho Corners.
Lord, "The Washington Post" march!
We did that one. We did it good.
Now the music is fading, fading away.
I can no longer hear my clarinet.
Well, it's over again, yes, again.
And too soon, much too soon,
forgotten me will disappear
under wet maple leaves,
trampled by an oom-pah tuba player.
I could just almost cry.
I walk slowly up Illinois Street.
I don't feel like doing nothing.

ALEX WRIGHT
Opera House

The last old building
to be torn down
on East Lincoln Street
was Opera House.
It was snowing quite hard
all day yesterday
and the work crew
knocked off early.
The building
was still standing
when school let out,
and some of us guys
and Pearl and Beth and Dawn
went inside
for one more
magic show,
two more encores
of "Old Man River,"
and the third act
of *Our Town.*
This afternoon
the Opera House
was all gone.
Yes, it was gone.
Gone, gone, gone.
Pearl grabbed my arm.
I could feel her nails
bite through my shirt.
There was nothing to do
but pick up a brick
for a souvenir
and carry it back home
to West Lincoln Street.

CLAIRE LANCASTER
Ice and Snow

The snow falls
in big, soft flakes
on the river,
yes, the water
is still frozen,
though it is
the second week in March
and anybody
in this town
who mentions
with a salesman's grin
that spring is almost here
is greeted with
a cough, a frown,
a sneer, an oath,
a silent stare,
but still the snow
is pretty falling
on the river,
and because
I'm not working today
I bend over
the highway bridge
and smile a bit
as the flakes
kiss me on my ear,
fall on my jacket,
melt in my hair,
and I'm glad
we're not done
with winter's long
circus of snow.

ISABEL OGDEN
Redneck

Faith, honey,
don't worry
your pretty
head none, your
father is
not some poor,
downtrodden
redneck. He
works at the
bank and takes
an hour for
lunch. Forget
about your
Grandpa and
your Grandma.
Now *they* were
rednecks, and
Uncle Zeke
too, I guess.
We've come a
long way from
old Cobbtown,
Georgia, let
me tell you.
Now help me
put these pink
slipcovers
on these chairs
and then I'll
play you a
tune on the
bass fiddle
that will make
you want to
dance a jig
and which will
put smiling
thoughts in your
pretty head,
Faith, honey.

JACQUELINE NERVAL
Trash

Sister Rose is reading trash again.
Her eyes are feasting
on erotic words.
A sticky breeze
stirs her short, wavy hair.
I put my schoolbooks
on the hall table,
where there are red grapes
in a wooden bowl
and a pair of black lace panties.
Sister Rose is reading trash again.
Some racy book she found somewhere
or wasted cash for.
She doesn't see me.
She doesn't hear me.
I eat fourteen grapes.
They taste both sour and sweet.
On the blue wall
the antique clock clucks
like a mother hen.
Sister Rose is reading trash again.

BUDDY AZZOLINA
Suicide Note

Last week
you told
the Fuller Brush man
I was
sick.

Yesterday
you told
the butcher
I had
AIDS.

Today
you can tell
the undertaker
I am
dead.

FRANCES BELLAMY
White Man's Flies

I'm sure by now
you should know that
bees were introduced
to the Middle West
by white settlers.
"Them white man's flies,"
said the Indians.
But a fly never
zapped me like the bee
I, barefoot in
the clover grass,
stepped on today.
I know there once
was some Indian,
some Wyandot,
Kickapoo, or Fox,
who did the same thing.
"Damn white man's flies,"
he must have said.
"Them everywhere,
just like white man."
The settlers of course
called them honeybees
or bumblebees.
They'd tiptoe around
and take their honey
with utmost care.
Bumbling, blind me,
I didn't take care,
didn't watch my step.
First, the stab of pain,
then swelling, then
the itch and scratch.
White man's flies, my foot!

RITA OBERKFELL
Eight O'clock in the Evening

I was shaving my legs.
I wanted them smooth as glass.

"Well, how's the world?" he said.

"Late this afternoon
three sparrows
dust-bathed themselves
in the sharp curve
of my driveway," I said.

"Well, what of it?" he said.

"Nothing at all, I guess.
I just thought
you probably
never noticed
things like that," I said.

"Well, who's got time?" he said.

I wanted them smooth as glass.
I was shaving my legs.

SYLVESTER F. BILLINGS
The Civil War

Jess, when you fell on that icy playground
and broke your leg in three places
they took you to Alliance Community Hospital,
and when they let you out
you were wearing a big white cast
on which all of your school chums
wrote their names and get-well messages,
and you could not play basketball anymore,
nor skate on the pond with Rhoda Collins,
and so you moped around the house for awhile
until you finally settled down with a book
and started reading about Abe Lincoln and Jeff Davis
and General Sherman and General Grant
and about the Army of the Cumberland
and the Army of Northern Virginia
and about the Battle of Missionary Ridge
and the siege of Vicksburg
and about the 2nd Iowa and the 52nd Illinois
and Andersonville and Appomattox,
and before we knew it
there was another Civil War buff
in the Sylvester F. Billings family,
and that suits us just fine,
because from now on, my son,
when we speak of The War under this roof
you will know full well
of which war we are talking about.

HELEN ABERNATHY
Animal Shelter

Poor Buster wouldn't eat much.
He seemed to lose his appetite.
Then we found him dead,
out on the main highway,
hit by some car or truck,
the overhead streetlight swinging
in the cold midnight wind.
We buried him in the backyard,
next to three cats, a rabbit,
and a rooster named Roger.
The dog was a good pet.
He was no trouble at all.
He was homely, as bulldogs are,
had a fine disposition,
was affectionate and gentle as fog.
When our son, Jed, got real sick
and the doctor said leukemia
would take him from us soon,
we let the boy have a dog.
We took him to the animal shelter,
that humane prison for the homeless.
He passed up the cute mutts,
the clear-eyed terriers,
the soft-eared spaniels,
the eager-nosed beagles.
So we brought home Buster
with the drool, the slight limp,
the face like a bad earthquake.
Jed died in my arms last March.
"Does God love Buster?" he said,
just before the end came.
"Yes, he does, very much," I said.
"That's good, Mama," he said.
"And he loves you, Jed," I said.
"I know," Jed said. "I know."
Then three weeks later
Buster came to his end, too.
What more is there to say?
A boy, a dog, good friends
who were happy to be alive,

to be in one another's company.
They taught us to love quickly,
to love what we love to love
for as long as we can cling
to this hazardous, haphazard life.

GILBERT HUTCHINSON
Toilet Paper

When I ran out of toilet paper
in the middle of the night,
my bowels aching for action,
and stared out the bathroom window
and saw my neighbor's tree
thoroughly toilet papered,
by some highjinks prankster
or youthful gang of screwballs,
I knew things had gone awry,
my life now turned bizarre.
The tree was a minor disaster,
there in the streetlight's glare.
I couldn't smile, couldn't laugh.
The bathroom is a sober room.
Serious things are done there.
Man, I had to take a crap.

ERIKA FONTANA
Parties

Don't mention
my eighth
birthday party.
That was when
nobody came
at all
and I cried
and Mom swore
and Dad he
threatened
to move us
clear out of town
he was so
doggone mad.
It wasn't
until
I was twelve
that I worked up
enough nerve
to ask for
one more
birthday party.
Mom invited
thirty-two
boys and girls
and thirty came.
A lamp
was knocked over
and a goldfish
died under
the sofa.
So Dad he
threatened
to leave town
again.
But Mom and I
we just laughed
and laughed
we were so
happy.

LUCILLE SCRIBNER
Diary

The only reason
my five-year diary
looks so tacky,
like rats have been
nibbling on
the blue-lined pages,
is because
I ripped out all
the pages I wrote
about him, about
William John Newhouse.
I've had a huge crush
on him for two years,
ever since he moved
to this town
from Shelbyville,
Indiana.
But he has never
paid attention
to me at all.
I always thought that
sooner or later
he would shine
his blue eyes my way.
What's happened now is
that he has asked
my very best friend,
Anita Kees,
to go with him to
the school spring picnic.
I can't stand it.
No, I can't take it.
So, as I said,
I tore out
those hot pages
where I wrote about
his bashful smile,
his sexy legs,
his chest muscles,

364

and about the cute
black hairs that grow
around his navel.
I said to myself,
"Billy John, you're dead,
bang, bang, bang."
I crumpled up
the diary pages
and put them into
a garbage bag,
pushing them under
some egg shells
and some coffee grounds.
I said to myself,
"Gone, good riddance."
Then I changed my mind
and fished out
the garbage-stained sheets
and read them again
and took them to bed
and put them under
my pillow.
I couldn't sleep.
I moved my hand
to my groin
which was moist with
the old excitement
I still feel for
William John Newhouse
from Shelbyville,
Indiana.

OZZIE NAVARRO
Just the Facts

I'm a Sunflower County lawyer.
My son lives in a war-surplus tent.
I collect railroad timetables and souvenirs.
My daughter works in a nursing home.
I've published a pamphlet on raccoons.
My common-law wife is Yugoslavian.
I dropped out of six colleges in six years.
My first love was from Xenia, Ohio.
I hang Chagall on my office walls.
My favorite colors are black and white.
Big business scorns the blue-collar worker.
I always defend the county's poor people.
Some folks can't pay me a thin dime.
It's the unions that have saved the common man.
I once owned a tangerine Volvo.
I also like the work of Miró and Matisse.
My first love was a nymphomaniac.
It was at Duke I earned my law degree.
My common-law wife eats olives in bed.
All raccoons are misunderstood.
My daughter reads poems to old women.
The trains of my youth were always friendly.
My son wants to move to a treehouse.
I'm a Sunflower County lawyer.

BONNIE ARNELL
A Motherless Child

These are the names of our cats:
Muggins, Chico, and Pokey.

We had balloons for my birthday party.
Daddy dressed up like a falling-down clown.
Melissa stuck candy corn in her nose.
I blew out all eight candles on my cake.
Uncle Walt scared us with a ghost story.
Nadine said, "Bonnie has got no mother."
I sneaked off upstairs and cried my eyes out.

These are the names of our cats:
Alfie, Coco, and Taffy.

Today I couldn't picture Mother good.
I went quickly and looked at my snapshot.
She's standing alone on a green mountain.
Mother liked roses, movies, and pizza.
I was at Chandi Budd's house when she died.
Daddy drove over there and brought me home.
Some girls never seem to run out of tears.

These are the names of our cats:
Guido, Caleb, and Freddie.

NOLA GARRISON
Composition

At the Friday
fish fry at Gene's
Bar and Grill up
on North Fifth Street
I heard nothing
and saw nothing
worth writing down
in my notebook,
nothing funny,
nothing bizarre,
no one petting
in a parked car.
No, the words were
boring, the dull
faces empty
as the soup bowls
back in Gene's white
kitchen, so I
have decided
to try the gas
station in the
morning and the
chirpy, chitchat,
"We don't cash checks
and the bank don't
serve meals" Elite
Cafe at noon,
because, because
somebody here
in Alliance
must be saying,
must be doing
something I can
use in a short
story for Miss
Cooper's class in
composition.
I don't want much
and don't need much

from so and so
or such and such.
I'm looking for
little things, just
a few little
small-town things that
will put words in
my head and then,
hopefully, words
on this blank and
blinding paper.

SALLY WHIPPLE
Great Grandmother's Speech on New Year's Eve

I didn't say I wasn't going.
I said maybe I won't be going.
But a party's a party,
so to go is to keep going.
And I aim to keep going.

Old man, get me my shoes.

MILDRED CESAREK
At the Crossroads

I sit in the kitchen and wind my watch.

Above this crossroads store
Grandma can't fry eggs anymore.

She's buried in a graveyard box,
north wind blowing around her name,
a shovel propped against a tilted stone.

Sleet rattles in the withered corn.

Lying upside down on a pink platter of pins
is Grandma's silly looking Easter hat.
Because Suzy cries when she sees it now,
I hide it in the cellar behind the onion sack.

Pine trees are stiff with thick ice.

There have been too many griefs here,
too many ghosts whose graves I know,
too many eyes that stare at mine.

Above this crossroads store
Grandma can't crochet anymore.

I will mourn her best I can.

KATHY SCHOONOVER
Foreign Affairs

Last night I read
that the Russian
people love to
eat cucumbers
and that Finnish
is the most un-
pronounceable
language in the
world, and I said
to my grandson,
who was sitting
in his high chair,
with baby food
spread all over
his lunchtime face,
"I don't like cu-
cumbers and I
know you don't like
them, either, right?"
and my grandson
crumpled his wet
soda cracker
and said something
so garbled, so
nonsensical
he could have been
speaking Finnish,
for all I know.

GREGORY DAWSON
Sick Before Supper

What they did was to serve bad booze,
the cheap bourbon, the bargain gin.
Anyway, when it came time to eat,
only three of us could get there
to dine on shrimp cocktails and big T-bone steaks.
Neil was on his knees by the toilet bowl.
Peter and Sharon were out by the pump.
Carla was lying down on the couch,
moaning about strange tasting hors d'oeuvres.
But it wasn't the food, nothing we ate.
It was the cut-rate hooch that did us dirt.
We drank too much of it, of course.
It was that kind of party, that kind of group.
Some folks don't mix with some folks, that's all.
Now if I can just stop being sick,
here in the yard, bending over a tall weed,
I'm going to go straight on home
and pour myself a decent scotch.

DEENA FERACA
Child Molester

I was getting
rained on real good
and the ink smeared
on the top part
of my essay
about lambs which
was sticking out
of my math book
when a maroon
and tan car stopped
at the curb and
this man pushed his
face up toward the
open window
and said "Get in
little girl and
I'll drive you to
your school" and I
almost did I
was so soaked by
then but when he
smiled at me and
I saw his sharp
yellow teeth and
big greasy nose
I said "No thanks"
and began to
run a little
splashing through the
muddy puddles
on the sidewalk
to my school which
was still two more
blocks down Sixth Street
and Marla told
the teacher what
had happened and
she telephoned
to the police

who picked him up
four days later
near the high school
but I can't say
what they did to
him and for four
weeks my dad drove
me to school rain
or shine and I
still get scared when
I remember
how that wolf man
looked at me and
I cried again
last night before
I tried my best
to go to sleep.

JILL CORBETT
Rocking Horse

Much more than anything
that's fun to do,
I love to ride and rock
my rocking horse.
When Daddy comes home
and puts on one of his
loud bebop jazz records,
I ride faster and faster.
I don't want to get off
when Mom calls me to supper
or when it's time for bed.
Tuesday is tomorrow.
I wish I could gallop
my rocking horse
past my old stupid school
and yell to my friends,
"Listen to me now.
This is Jill Corbett.
I'm not coming today.
I'm riding my horse."

KIRK GEARHART
Diesels

Another diesel truck swooshes
down Potawatomi Road.
I hear fallen leaves scrape
against the street bricks.
Tomorrow is moving day
to another house
and I can't sleep a wink.
The sound of a big rig
plunging through the night
was something I used to like.
But not anymore.
One slid off an icy highway
last January
up near Red Wing, Minnesota.
My brother Dale was in it,
hitchhiking to St. Cloud
to see his new girlfriend.
He's gone, gone, gone, gone.
I sure wish I could tell him
I'm out for football again
and that I lost his
last silver dollar
somewhere in the dead leaves
on the edge of town.

RUSSELL HAYES
Federal Highway

"Gone," he said.
"What's gone?" I said.
"It won't never be the same," he said.
"What won't never?" I said.
"The farm, the farm," he said.
"My god, what's gone wrong?" I said.
"They ran a federal highway through it," he said.
"Then gone is what it is," I said.
"Oh, it's still there," he said.
"But you aren't there," I said.
"That's right," he said.
"It's just not no place to farm now," I said.
"No, it ain't," he said.
"Then you're gone for good?" I said.
"Gone," he said.

LUTHER WILHELM
Nightmare

She was engaged to Tom Marsh
and she shouldn't have done it,
and I shouldn't have done it.
But we did it.
Sue Ann and I did it.
We went sledding on the long, steep hill
at Hodge's Mound.

He was jealous of Sue Ann Crawford,
but he shouldn't have done it.
But he did it.
Tom did it.
He hijacked a county snowplow
and ran over Sue Ann at the end of the hill
at Hodge's Mound.

I was enraged at Tom Marsh
and I shouldn't have done it.
But I did it.
I beat Tom's head against a big rock
until he lay dead
at the far side of the darkening hill
at Hodge's Mound.

CYNTHIA RAINES
Silent

In my shook up,
glass-ball childhood
I was silent as
a Basque sheepherder
in a snowstorm.
My parents were so eager
to get me to say something,
to say anything,
that if I made any kind
of noise with my mouth,
they would ask me,
"What did you say?"
And I would tell them,
"Nothing. I was
clearing my throat."
"Oh," they would say.
"Oh what?" I would say.
"Nothing," they would say.
"Oh," I would say,
then walk away.

PORTER KNOX
The Christmas Tree

Above Sam Kuykendall's dime store a loudspeaker blares
a never-ending selection of Christmas carols.

O little town of Bethlehem
How still we see thee lie,
Above thy deep and dreamless sleep
The silent stars go by.

Years ago, when I was the head of a large family,
before everyone either died or moved away for good,
we always had a brightly-lit scotch pine or balsam fir
at Christmastime on the farm near Noon Prairie.
I remember the avalanche of presents, the happy faces,
the huge turkey dinners with candlelight and wine.

I shouldn't have done it, I guess, but I did it.
I went out into the teeth of a zero-cold wind,
walked up to the Christmas tree man at the A&P,
stamped my freezing feet in the icy parking lot,
and demanded to buy the biggest tree for sale,
having found thirty dollars in the tobacco-tin bank.
Oh, I had to have a Christmas tree on Christmas Eve,
and I was willing to leave a sick bed to get one,
willing to drag it back to my room on Illinois Street.

I will have to string popcorn to decorate my tree.
I have neither time nor strength to search for lights
or red and green balls or the soiled blue angel.
My old man's hands flutter like wounded quail.
I puff my pipe, cough, then slump to the floor.
A newspaper catches fire and the popcorn and the tree.

Still in thy dark night shineth
The everlasting light,
The hopes and fears of all the years
Are met in thee tonight.

The fire engine screams through the tinseled streets.
Now no one can hear "Silent Night, Holy Night."

MILTON CAVANAUGH
Scratch

The blue fingernail moon
is a scratch on the 2 a.m. sky.
There's nothing quite so strange
as empty downtown streets.
Instead of thinking how peaceful,
I think of the big bomb.
Goodbye crummy storefronts.
Never again doughnut shop.
Gone for good old pot of a courthouse.
Real estate as unreal estate.
A mountain of red bricks.
One more left turn and I'm home.
The crickets sing wildly
till I hit the back door.
From her wicker basket by the stove,
the calico cat ignores me,
refuses to blink good morning.
I climb the stairs, shoes in hand,
and tiptoe into the bedroom.
My wife, naked, snoring loudly,
lies curled up on her right side,
her bony left hip riding high
in the air-conditioned air.
I empty my pockets on the chest:
two quarters, half a cheap cigar,
blue chalk from the poolroom.
I take off my clothes and lie down
on my stretch of the bed.
I can't bowl worth a shit,
can't cop a game of pool.
I run my hand across my cheek
and trace the long, thin scratch
my wife put there last weekend
when I told her, without a smile,
"Your body is not too bad, I guess.
It's just that you've had it so long."
We're edgy now we've turned sixty,
worried about lack of money,
our old-age aches and pains,
not knowing how it's going to go.

CHRISTINE ANDREWS
Company Lunchroom

The Hispanic girl,
who last Tuesday
between two forklifts
showed me her
butterfly tattoo,
has just now taken
her enchilada
out of the new
lunchroom microwave
and sits across
the table from me.
Now that's a fine
noontime feed.
Gosh, it smells good.
I struggle with my
baloney sandwich,
wash it down
with Mountain Dew.
I wonder what
she'll eat tomorrow?
Yesterday I had
egg salad on white
and some stale
potato chips.

KERMIT OLMSTED
Roots

"We're staying right here the rest of our lives," I said.
"In Illinois?" she said.
"That's where we are, isn't it?" I said.

CALVIN FAIRBANKS
Letter to Grandma

Mother says
I haven't
written you
in five years
but I never
had nothing to say
until
now
that is
and I'm just busting
to tell you
we saw
Adolph Hitler's
personal
armored
bullet-proof
car.

We were over
to the fair
and there it was
and was I surprised
I didn't
expect
nothing
like that
to turn up
among all those
pigs and pickles
Jimmy didn't
neither
wow-eeee
how are you Gram
love
Cal.

REGINA WASHINGTON
Incompatibility

After working all morning long in my
sad-rag and mop-flop kitchen,
I said to myself, I said, "Woman,
you've got to lie down
before you just plain fall down."
So on the daybed in the dining room
I stretched out on the spread.
Outside, the squirrels
ran up the tree trunks
and the tall weeds grew taller.
I must have slept at least an hour,
and when I awoke I knew
the awful, terrible truth,
the painful, headline truth.
I knew I'd rather look
at a sink full of dirty dishes
than look at him, my husband.
When I tell Norman the news,
I'll say "incompatibility."
What I won't say is that
during my afternoon nap
on the daybed of housewife dreams
I heard the weeds say his name
and felt the flying feet of squirrels
dig into my broom-tired bones.

LOLA FOWLES
Guitar Strings

In
the
little
country
graveyard
south
of
town
I
found
guitar
strings
under
an
oak
tree
three
lonesome
guitar
strings
ripped
from
the
loins
of
a
moist
and
star
crossed
summer
love.

JACY LAMONICA
Coy

Bart Kindlesparger
is a bodybuilder
with huge muscles everywhere.
Right this minute he is
sitting on our davenport
in his skimpy blue shorts.
He and Brother Biff
are watching a boxing match
on cable television.
I can't take my eyes off
this bulging blue vein
that runs almost the length
of Bart's hefty right thigh
and then disappears under
the edge of his shorts.
It looks like a blue highway
on a gas station map
or a rain-swollen creek
on a stretch of bronze prairie.
It is driving me wild,
getting me all sexed up.
During a commercial break,
Bart turns his eyes on me.
"Jacy, you want to go
fishing on Sunday?" he says.
Now, I'd walk on thumbtacks
to be alone in a boat
or sit on a riverbank
with that gorgeous body,
but I don't want to seem
too eager, too zealous.
"I guess so," I say.
He shoots me a bashful smile.
"Just you and me," he says.
I nibble my finger.
"Sure," I say. "Why not."

ELMER PRATT
Revelation

Though she quailed from me,
by dribbles and drabbles I wormed
the cold truth out of her.

She had sinned, and by god
there would be repentance or I
was no Christian father at all.

The nerve of her telling us
that she was going to a school play,
then going instead to a gin mill.

Her story was very roundabout, but
I could smell the booze,
knew male hands had crawled her flesh.

I took off my leather belt,
pulled her panties below her knees,
and let her have it good.

Though she wailed and pled,
I could not stop smacking those
white and plump and lovely buns.

The more my passion grew,
the more confused I got.
Then she wrenched away from me.

Oh, how quickly it comes upon you
that your child is no longer child
but a woman, woman fleshed.

ADELAIDE CRAWFORD
Initiation

They told me because I
was new in their town,
and even though they liked me
well enough to play with me
after school and weekends,
they had to do something to me
I wasn't going to like,
and this boy named Bubba
took this big hairy rope
and tied me up to a tree
and he said not to cry
or yell or scream for help,
and this girl named Georgia
unbuttoned my white jeans
and then yanked them down
all the way to my shoe tops,
and they smeared gobs of mud
on my cheeks and forehead
and on my bare legs too,
and then they left me there
and I stayed there until
an old man and a young nun
got out of their antique car
and untied the rope,
which was hurting my stomach,
and I pulled up my muddy pants
and ran real fast to my house,
where Mom and Dad were still
rearranging tables and chairs,
and said to my brother,
"I don't think we're going to
like this town very much."

CURTIS LURTSEMA
National Pastime

Baseball is a game I know something about, boy.
I've played ball for forty years or more:
with a truck driver who hated trucks,
with my grandpa of the Dizzy Dean chatter,
with a Canadian who swore in Spanish,
with a pot smoker from Madison, Wisconsin,
with a shoe clerk who always fell down,
with a thirteen-year-old Vietnamese kid,
with a prostitute named Eva,
with my uncle Barney of the busted bat,
with a conductor off the Rock Island Lines,
with a hotshot fertilizer salesman,
with a semipro who lived over the grocery store,
with a 200-pound lady wrestler,
with a dwarf who came to town with the circus,
with a farmer's daughter out of Fayette County,
with a bozo who once met Vince DiMaggio,
with my dad of the roundhouse curve,
with a steam fitter who would rather drink gin,
with a one-eyed guy with no eyebrows,
with a friend who wore a Pirates cap,
with a beanpole who starred for Bradley U,
with a girl I got married to,
with my brother of the head-first slide,
with a cop who swiped my catcher's mitt.
I've played ball in April rain and August heat.
I've played with snow on the ground
and when fall leaves blew across second base.
Hey, it's good news you got yourself a glove.
We will have to toss a few after lunch.
Or right now, if you can wait to eat.

BUCKY ATWOOD
  Coming Down

My brother flew my butterfly kite
the very afternoon I bought it.
Got out of his car, said, "Give me that."
He had just come home from work,
another bum day selling Ford cars,
still wearing his clip-on bow tie,
his shirttail hanging out of his pants.
Said, "Watch how an old pro handles it."

Mom and Dad were inside, talking about
the light bill, the gas bill, the phone bill.

The kite went up higher, higher, higher.
My brother's sky-blue eyes shone like stars.
He is a perfect wizard with kites.
After awhile he got tired of watching
this piece of dancing green springtime.
Said, "Here, hold onto the string, squirt,"
and went to his room upstairs
and turned on the light over his bed.
When it began to get really dark,
I hauled in the string fast as I could.
The kite came down, down, down, down
and got stuck in our black walnut tree.
I screamed, I cursed, then I cried.
My brother ran outside and told me,
"Coming down is the hard part."

Mom and Dad were inside, talking about
the light bill, the gas bill, the phone bill.

Last week we moved to a smaller house.
We handled everything ourselves.
Three loads in a big rented truck.
Northwestern Mutual Life let Dad go.
Called him in, said, "We want you to resign."
Though he's tried, he can't find work.
Mom is not talking to Dad now.
My kite is still in the walnut tree.

ROSCOE VAUGHAN
All Things to All People

Once again I'm trying
to not be all things to
all people, but then I
get involved in a rap
session on game hunting,
which I hate, at the post
office and stick my two
cents in and say, "Well, right,
deer, yes, but take pheasants.
Now there's some kind of fun.
I was one time out in
central South Dakota—"
And all the guys smile and
nod and I know they think
I'm a real hunter just
like them. But when the State
Farm agent gives me his
card and a small pocket
calendar and says, "I'll
give you a buzz next time
I go out for rabbits,"
I stammer, "Oh, I'd—I'd
like—like that," and then I
fool with my mail and say,
"See you gents later" and
walk up Main Street to my
wife who still thinks I like
to color Easter eggs.

ERIN KAISER
North Woods

There's little hope
Grandfather will
go with us now
to the cabin
in Wisconsin.
The worn-out map
of his face and
those tired eyes say
quite plainly he
would rather not
be urged to leave
here for up there.
You see, he's old.
His roads are closed.
His bridge is out.
He's of no mind
to see again
what he's seen so
many times, and
my telling him
about the big
fish he could catch
from boat or dock
does not stir up
the sand grains of
his silted mind
or make him smile
as in summers
before his stroke.
So if he won't
go, he won't go.
I'll not force him.

SHELDON MERCER
Common Sense

At the
little
greasy
spoon up
from the
mainline
tracks the
tall black
brakeman
puts down
his first
after
work beer
and says
his dad
told him
only
a rich
man or
a fool
votes Re-
publi-
can and
that his
dad was
surely
right and
he would
never
be rich
and that
he would
be damned
if he
would vote
like a
poor fool.

395

GLORIA HAWTHORNE
Her Dying Child

River is choked with sand.
Stacy limps down Pine Street.
This sun-baked September.
Crop duster dusting crops.
That cat, that tree, that stone.
She loves what she can touch.
Wine from the vine is mine.
Old bumbling bumblebee.
Stacy sprawls on pale grass.
My heart hums a slow tune.

ARNOLD WHEELER
Ambition

The big white house on Harvester Street.
Back home again for another Christmas.
We sit before a feisty log fire.
Pyramids of presents, boxes, wrapping paper.
Talk of what he got, what she got.
Brag of what money can buy.
Then they turn their tongues on me.
"What do you study at college?" Father says.
"Gauguin and Van Gogh," I say.
"What is your favorite subject?" Mother says.
"Modigliani," I say.
"Just what *do* you get out of school?" Father says.
"How to draw the nude," I say.

"What do you want to be?" Father says.
"See that maple tree over there?" I say.
"Yes, I see it. So what?" Father says.
"Well, that's what I want to be," I say.
"Trees don't do a damn thing," Father says.
"Now you've got the idea, Pop," I say.

"I just want to loaf and invite my soul," I say.
"What's this rubbish about a soul?" Father says.
"It never comes up in the gas business," I say.

By the time another Christmas comes calling,
I'm living in a cold rented room,
two thousand miles from cozy home and hearth.
"How come a bright fellow like you
is working nights loading trucks?"
my landlady says, dialing down the heat,
reaching for another sweater.
"Why don't you show more ambition?"
"Andy Warhol," I inform her,
hoping she will change the subject.

PHOEBE YAEGER
Cheerleader

Feeling
kind of
crazy
this af-
ternoon
before
the big
game with
Central,
I wiped
my face
and knees
with a
monarch
butter -
fly. Now
when I
jump a-
round and
do cart-
wheels, I
sweat our
school col-
ors: orange
and black.
Go team.
Fight team.
Go. Go.
Fight. Fight.

398

LEONARD MASSINGAIL
Fatherly Advice

You don't know beans about girls
and you are going about half-cocked.
It will always be a wild-goose chase
until, by hook or crook,
you break the ice with her.
She'll let you cool your heels
as long as you beat about the bush.
It's no skin off my nose
if you can't cut the mustard
and act like a fish out of water.
I'm not talking through my hat
when I say you're asleep at the switch.
Getting a doll is no lead-pipe cinch,
and coming down with a case of cold feet
puts romance on the rocks.
She sure looks like the real McCoy,
so make hay while the sun shines.
Get yourself in the groove, son.
Go the whole hog, right now.
I'd sweat my good blood
to rule the roost with that chick.
Just be a chip off the old block
and you'll soon be on Easy Street.
If you're going to hem and haw,
I'm going to be madder than a wet hen.
Look, either fish or cut bait,
or you will always eat crow.
Damnit, take the bull by the horns!

CLAUDE ROSE
Deluge

The rain that was
predicted for
early morning
finally came
this afternoon
and the deluge
was something to
really marvel
over as was
the piercing scream
of this girl who
all the neighbors
said was wild as
a woodchuck and
a bit nutty
in the noodle
and who dashed up
the stone steps of
our wide front porch
and said she was
scared of lightning
and could she wait
out the storm with
me and I told
her I would love
her company
and she tied her
soaked pooch to a
porch post and came
over to me
where I sat on
a rattan chair
and made herself
cozy on my
lap which was all
right and I knew
she had nothing
on under her
flimsy cotton
dress and that was

all right too I
guess and she put
her sweaty arms
around my neck
and squeezed me tight
and I looked for
someone to get
me out of this
predicament
and her weight got
heavier and
heavier and
she said I was
her real daddy
and kissed me and
I prayed for the
rain to stop and
it did and she
got off my lap
and skipped down the
street with her dog
who threw back his
head and howled like
a wolf when the
strong and steamy
sun broke through the
gray clouds again.

KATE PINCHOT
Public Library

Books, books, books, books, books, books.
A dark, nasty Wednesday library night.
Tarkington, Thackeray, Tolstoy.
Big splash of rain against high windows.
"Yes, Mr. Roodhouse, we've had too much rain."
Stacks of books to put away again.
Galsworthy, Glasgow, Graham Greene.
Kid in farm cap asks about Mickey Spillane.
Crumpled library card I can't read.
Awful old man asleep over his *Fortune*.
Wet copy of *The Tin Drum* falls off the desk.
"Overdue means just that: overdue."
Three teenage girls giggle near the rubber plant.
"I'll accept the stamp but not bubble gum."
James Joyce, Henry James, James Jones.
The magazine racks are a mess.
Table heaped with Cracker Jack boxes.
These kids come here to eat, not study.
Two smashed Milk Duds sink into the carpet.
Would sure love to swat that Rukenbrod boy.
Wendy Witherspoon is no angel, either.
"Five minutes to closing time, five minutes."
Books on anatomy, biology, chess.
Books on falconry, gourmet cooking, health.
"No, mam, George Eliot is not a man.
Neither is Joyce Kilmer a woman.
Well, it's not *my* fault, Mrs. Mott."
Baudelaire, Verlaine, Rimbaud.
Another complaint from right-wing nincompoop.
"Yes, *The Grapes of Wrath* is a great book."
Must wake up that old man real quick.
"Okay, that's it, everyone must go, at once."
New novels scream in their bright jackets.
The big dictionary chokes on its forgotten words.
Masters and Lewis sob on the back shelf.
Civil War books hum old battle songs.
Louisa May Alcott lays down and dies.
Lightning, thunder, pelting rain.

"Leave that magazine here, please."
Oh God, let me lock the door and get out, now.
This librarian is drowning in books.
Books, books, books, books, books, books.

RAYMOND HARPER
Clowns

After we got back from
the circus in Chicago,
we wanted to be
wild animal trainers.
But all the dogs and cats
we had around here
wouldn't play the game,
wouldn't be our
lions and tigers.
We couldn't even
capture any of them.
We chased them over
wood fences and stone walls,
down driveways,
through wide side yards,
up sycamore trees.
But it was no go.
We had little chairs
to protect ourselves
and long belts for whips,
but no animals
to practice on.
"Clowns," Baxter said.
"Let's be circus clowns."
"Yeah, clowns," Barrett said.
I hustled to the house
and got Mom's
lipstick and rouge
and her face powder
and some of Dad's
baggy pants and raggy coats.
"Clowns," I said when
I rejoined my friends.
"We'll be funny clowns,
real circus clowns.
Hard work but proud work."

MICKEY CONWAY
Tornado Warning

Tornado warning!
I snatch my shoe box of gum-dusty
bubble gum baseball cards
and hightail it to the cellar.
"What's so awful special
about those baseball cards?"
says my sister, pouting,
hugging a couple of overdressed dolls.
Mom fills three jelly glasses
with Country Time lemonade.
"Look here," I say,
"if the house blows down
with all our furniture and stuff,
I can start a new house with
Smoky Burgess and Ewell Blackwell,
Wally Post and Vada Pinson,
Harvey Haddix and Solly Hemus,
Curt Flood and Roy Face,
Mickey Vernon and Elmer Valo,
Eddie Joost and Larry Jackson,
Johnny Logan and Whitey Lockman."
My sister gives me a sour look.
Mom smiles, squeezes my arm.
I open the shoe box
and take out Richie Ashburn, who had
a lifetime batting average of .308.
"Not bad," I say, "not bad at all."
"Drink your lemonade," Mom says.
"Yeah, drink your lemonade,"
says my sister, putting shoes
on a prune-face doll.
This is the third time this month
we've been down here
with the sack of peat moss,
the busted-up croquet set,
and two years of old newspapers.
I want to tell you something.
I'm getting a bit tired of hearing
"tornado warning!"

PAMELA DOOLEY
Subdivision

As we found out weeks later,
when the truth came out,
the dozen red roses
delivered to our house
were meant for the teenage girl
who lived next door,
but when they arrived
there was no card with them
and my daughter quickly
put them in some water
and set them on the grand piano
and said to us,
"I know who they are from,"
but she wouldn't tell who,
and my son said to me,
"Mom, they're not for Allison,"
but he didn't say it
to his moony sister,
oh no, he didn't say it to her,
and a week after that,
when the roses were dying
and dropped their petals,
the girl next door broke up
with her boyfriend,
who got in his Mustang
and squealed the tires
all the way down the block,
and my husband said to me,
"What is going on here?"
and my daughter broke into
a cloudburst of tears
and slammed her bedroom door.

GOLDIE KLIPSTEIN
Creative Writing

My boy will never
know higher mathematics
or mechanical engineering,
and there's no Harvard
in his future, either,
no job making big money
in Houston
or Los Angeles,
for when I found
"Between two red barns,
corn stubble sticking up
above the snow:
ragged yellow candles
on a giant's
birthday cake"
typed on bond paper
and later printed
in the new *Catalpa Review*,
I knew he was a poet,
and thanked God
his father wasn't around
to see his only son
plunging wide-eyed
into creative writing.

BRENT PICCONY
Athlete

Two years ago
I was a junior
at Alliance High School,
a hotshot ballplayer,
a center fielder
with good speed,
a rocket arm,
and a batting average
of over .300.
Then along came
our big game with
archrival Central
and I couldn't play
because I was flunking
Physics and Biology.
We lost the game
by a couple of runs
and Coach Pine
was mad at me.
"Damn, Piccony,
we would have won
had you played," he said.
"Next year take only
the courses you can pass."
So I signed up for
Photography,
Home Economics,
and Floriculture
my senior year
and never missed
a single game.
I hit .426
that season
and we were champs.
Coach was very pleased.
He gave me a hug and said,
"You're great, my boy,
a real athlete.

Now take this film here
and make me
two 5 by 7s
of each of these pictures.
Then when you're done,
I'll take you out
for a big pizza supper
and introduce you
to my daughter Cindy."
I went right to
the school darkroom
and said to myself,
"You're ready for college.
You know the score,
how to play the game."

NANCY EASTWICK
Jericho Township

No one tells me where I was born.
Look, hawk shadow across white barn.
Pain of loss, pain of being lost.
Quick goodbye after sweat of lust.
Dying rabbit bleeds in blood dust.
Blue tractor cools off at blue dusk.
I want a tall horse, a gold coin.
Now who calls my name from fall corn?

KAREN HICKS
   Loony

That
woman
there
who
could
be
and
maybe
is
my
ancient
and
loony
aunt
from
Ko-
ko-
mo
rises
up
from
her
garden
in
bright
purple
shoes
and
bites
a
big
sun-
flower.

GWEN PETERSON
Sun Belt

All the sun and heat in
burnt-toast Arizona
was too much sun, too much
heat for those two to take,
and so they left it there
and came back home, returned
after six dry-tongued, old
cactus-boring, very
unshaded desert years.
Their features had become
a bit coarse, a bit tough.
It's the Hornsbys I am
talking about. Lorraine
and Henry B. Hornsby,
long-time residents of
Alliance, Illinois.
Before they got settled
in their cozy blue frame
house over on Locust
Street, Lorraine picked a big
hatful of red and gold
maple leaves off autumn's
green grass and spread them all
over her new dining
room table. Henry put
on his fur-lined jacket
and went to Ace Hardware
and bought a snowblower.
"Yuma, Phoenix, Tucson.
You can have those places.
Nothing but endless heat
waves, sunburn, wrinkled skin,
and the slurred speech of
the air-conditioning,"
Lorraine told us tonight.
"Good to be back," Henry
said, and dug some mittens
out of a shopping bag.

412

MAYBELLE JONES
A Trip to the Bank

It was the very yesterday.
We went to town again.

The bank had a cold bench.
My legs giggled me silly.

Mama whispered her mouth.
Spitty Baby grabbed tight.

We both had wet panties on.
I felt like an oyster, you know.

The man was full of money.
"Nice to meet you," I said.

Mama clicked her mushy purse.
We left with our smiles going.

A big sun wrinkled my eyes.
Dogs told naughty secrets.

Home was good to see.
But I forgot my beaded bag.

Mama said it wasn't funny.
Spitty Baby got spanked too.

Walks are nothing fun.
Now don't talk me into that.

413

JACK ERTEL
The Fighter

Nubs Lilly liked to use his fists.
A while back, during an overheated discussion
at our Saturday night poker session,
he, as usual, got in the first punch.
But it was also his last one,
because this gas-pump jockey named Jolly,
from over in Kendall County,
quickly laid him out with a nifty left hook.
Later, Nubs had to admit
that he had had enough of the fight game
and was not really another up-and-coming
"Two Ton Tony" Galento.

Now it's worse, for he's lifting weights
and talking all the time about Frank Gotch,
Hackenschmidt, and Stanislaus Zbyszco.
He fancies himself a wrestler, you see,
and all his cronies have grown very tired
of being asked to "go a fall or two."
Phil Graham says that if Nubs
keeps on flapping his big yap,
he's going to toss his ass into Park Street.
When I tell Nubs this latest bit of news,
he gives me a slow smile and says,
"Strangler Lilly spits on that kind of talk. "

EARL VAN HORNE
Monopoly

When Uncle Rex puts those big red hotels
on Boardwalk and Park Place,
it's all but over, and we know it.
He will bleed us bankrupt in no time.
So what does it matter if I own
all four railroads, the electric works,
Connecticut, Kentucky, North Carolina,
four houses on Baltic Avenue,
and an orange card to get me out of jail?

Pass me the peanut brittle, Paul.
And while you're at it, old man,
the rest of the clam dip too.

Anybody here for a round of dominoes
or a fast game of hearts?
Anybody for a long walk in the snow?

Come on, Olivia, put down the Ovaltine
and move your yellow doohickey
over to Marvin Gardens.

HAMILTON RIVERS
Noon at Carl's Mainline Cafe

Talk of septic tanks, sheep dip, soap powder.
Talk just to be talking, saying something:

"Claude says the water is more than four feet deep
in those corn bottoms south the highway bridge."

"I'm gonna sell my galvanized hay loader,
my metal detector, and my Star Wars bedspread."

"You say he's a duck decoy carver now
and you haven't seen him since last Arbor Day?"

"Joe Webb dropped dead after this evangelist fella
got him over excited and puking his guts."

"I sure guess it needs a new transmission, boy.
Why you can't even back that heap up anymore."

"He's a loud kid in Big Smith overalls.
Fergus is his name and it fits him to a T."

"Kay don't care much for her Kenmore washing machine.
Says never again another product from Sears."

"We cleaned out all that junk in the attic,
all them boxes with your forgotten toys in them."

"Me and Willie we used to get us free wienies
from Rukenbrod's store when we'd stop from school."

"I unwrapped it and it was waxed fruit.
Sister ain't had no sense since she gone to Tulsa."

"Leave me inform you them wienies were good.
Seems they was better tasting than cooked ones."

"It wasn't junk, it wasn't junk at all.
That was my Lionel train in there, you idiot."

"Ma's got herself an old Maytag, you know.
Pa he bought a platform rocker the very same day."

"Young Fergus is a pretty fair country jock,
but he bumbles about without benefit of brains."

"You was talkin' on rusty cars what leak.
We drove up here with water sloshing in the trunk."

"Ain't it sumpthing to go to your grave like that.
And Joe he never had a girl in bed or nothin'."

"I dropped Cousin Vera a card from Vero Beach.
It comes back stamped *Return to Sender.*"

"What I need is a double-oven electric range
and maybe some new oars for the rowboat."

"Well, that's our flood for this April.
That's about per usual for Sunflower County."

Damn, I wish I hadn't heard all that nonsense.
I don't even remember what the hell I ate.

WAYNE V. NOYES, JR.
Front Porch Swing

The old custom
of sitting
on the cozy
front porch swing
on a summer night
when dusk
smells like warm
clover grass
is not one
to tamper with
for when else does
a big pipe load
of Carter Hall
go so well
right after
a huge bowl
of strawberry
ice cream
and a ripe peach?

And maybe
close neighbors
with cold beer
and a banjo
will walk up
under the drooping
sycamore leaves
mosquitoes
stabbing
their sweaty
arms and necks
and we will
sing and swing
way beyond
the ten o'clock
news of the world
and who cares
if the rusty
joints creak?

JOYCE FENSTERMAKER
Sprinkler

It was the hottest hot day
of a hotter than hell summer.
We were all struck blind with sweat
and swimming with ice-cold drinks.
The bored neighborhood girls,
between eight and twelve years old,
plus my daughter, Shelley Bean,
who had turned thirteen that June,
wanted to get totally wet.
I hauled out the big sprinkler
we used to green-up the yard
when the grass got too brown
and put the spray on full force.
Such screams, such squeals of ecstasy.
Six landlocked mermaids
in their undershirts and underpants
grabbed and hugged each other.
Shiny bodies, floodtides of hair.
They got soaked as soaked can get.
Two girls showed off their small tits,
cherry tomatoes poking through
their clinging undershirts.
Shelley Bean thrust out apple breasts
and high-stepped around the yard.
She had gotten on my nerves all day
and I couldn't help myself.
I went and slapped her face hard.
She went bawling to the house.
I turned off the sprinkler.
The other girls went home.
That night, when the storm hit,
Shelley Bean climbed into my bed
for the first time in four years
and pressed her moist chest
against my sunburned back.
The storm raged on for an hour.
Wind and rain, lightning and thunder.
Shelley Bean clung tight to me
and we fell asleep that way,
drowning in our summer dreams.

419

IRA BRADFORD
Home from Work

I woke up
happy this
morning and
after orange
juice after
toast after
coffee I
wrote a short
entry in
my journal
in which I
said *Look don't
ever say
anything
bad against
snowstorms or
great blowing
blizzards that
come howling
out of the
Great Plains or
slippery
highways that
lead out of
town for you
are home and
don't have to
go to work
at that damn
tool and die
factory
today and
can finish
reading that
long book on
Eugene Debs
and begin
the one on
John Peter*

Altgeld and
I got dressed
as if it
were a good
Saturday
and not a
bad Wednesday
where I would
normally
be on my
feet for eight
hours of stress
discomfort
and boredom
if it were
not all white
and snowbound
outside and
I had one
more cup of
coffee with
cognac and
lit up a
big cigar.

LAUREL MADISON
Kids

Give your grandma
a kiss, children.
She's leaving now,
going home to
Massachusetts.
Come here, Leon.
Come here, Leslie.
A big kiss for
Grandma. She loves
you so much and
sends you presents
every year for
your birthday and
for Christmas too.
Leon, Leslie,
come here at once.
Your grandma's got
to say goodbye.
You may not see
her again for
a long, long time.
Well, then, a hug,
a real good hug,
then, for Grandma.
Oh, for god's sake,
you little brats,
give your grandma
a nice handshake.
Hey, that's the least
you can do. Shit.

GRADY SULLIVAN
Mourning Dove

Because of some kind of strange mishap,
perhaps a wrong way flight into
some much too shiny window,
mourning dove is put into a cage.
It's a matter of feathers.
One wing has little to fly with.
Mourning dove is safe in the house.
He needs our protection, our pity.
My son George will take care of him:
food, water, a branch to sit on.
Mourning dove hops around, looks mad,
wants to get back to sky and tree.
"Turn the poor thing loose," my wife says.
"No, no, don't do that," I say.
Mourning dove has a real name now.
George is going to call him Chester.
When he can fly, at least a bit,
we'll give this bouncing bird his freedom.
But until that feathered day,
mourning dove stays in the cage.

JONI LEFEVRE
  Bicycle Ride to the Cannery

Hot, hot, hot morning. Hate like shit to steam up so
quick. Worm-slimy sun. Knees pumping. Old wreck of a beat
bicycle. Face sweaty. Sticky thighs. Swimming is
where I want to be. Maybe nude at Potter's Pond.
Bobby equals sex. Ronald equals skinny prick.
Like big everything. Damn pothole. Fuck truck. Must cut
my long hair. Strip. Cold shower. Massage my rubber-hard
nipples. Bigger than Beverly's. Roger's stiff cock
when he walked away. Milo's muscles. Curly weeds.
Pubic itch. Cannery again. One more all-day
date with peas and beans. Oh hell's burnt carrots. I want
icy drinks. Bare feet. Windchimes on a shady porch. Not
this devil's trip to a summer-rotting jail. Crap.

WALTER INGRAM
In the Middle of the Middle West

Often on hot, humid summer nights,
if I am bored or terribly lonely,
I like to rip up the backcountry roads,
pushing my big blue Buick until she bounces
past corncrib, windmill, and cow barn.
But I also like to just creep along
and look into a lighted farmhouse
where the family is reading the news,
watching television, or playing cards,
or where a boy in a Cubs baseball cap
is tacking a pennant to his bedroom wall,
or where, hopefully, a pretty girl
is walking the kitchen floor in her slip.
It is then I start to glow,
to feel affectionate toward people again.

But this evening I have had too much gin.
The katydids are shrilling in the darkness.
And I am fresh out of love.

The roads, the farms, the good folks
who live on those islands in the corn
will have to wait for that other me.

Damn, it is hard to stay sober here
when one day yawns into the next
and there is little nerve left
to scale the fence, fly the coop.

The Buick sulks under the sullen leaves.

I pass out in my overstuffed chair.

I am being buried half alive
among the tired smiles of used-car salesmen
in the middle of the Middle West.

HUGH WITT
Doorbell

After a lunch
of pork and beans,
six black olives,
and half a can
of fruit cocktail,
I answered the
doorbell to a
young man who told
me the world was
going to end
in ten days and
was I prepared
to make peace with
Brother Jesus?
and I laughed and
said, "I'm having
enough trouble
staying on some
kind of speaking
terms with brothers
Rex and Leroy,"
and he ran his
long, bony hand
through his homemade
haircut and said,"
"It's no joking
matter," so I
took his pamphlet
that described all
the dark things to
come and went right
to my study
and lit my pipe
and made myself
a double Jack
Daniel's and said
to the cat, "You
better get off
your furry butt,

it may be much
later than we
think, and I don't
know about you,
kid, but I still
have some living
I ain't lived yet."

KIRBY QUACKENBUSH
September Moon

The old houses, dusted with moonshine,
creak in the dry and dragging wind
that pokes about this town,
where potato salad and cold beans
are eaten in stuffy kitchens,
where, in tubs of tepid water,
ponytailed girls who love fast horses
slide pink soap between their thighs,
where skinny boys lift weights
in bedrooms gaudy with football stars,
where doctors read comic books
and lawyers read numbers on checks,
where sex-starved wives wait in the nude
for tipsy husbands to be bored
with beer glass and cue stick,
where children sleep like stones
and hall clocks tick and tock
and cats yowl and dogs growl,
as another hot Labor Day winds down
in the webbed and wrinkled dark,
and I, moondust on my face,
return from a long walk to the depot,
the depot of many fierce goodbyes,
and it's just this I want to say,
"Luanne, my lost and lonely girl,
if you want me on this summer night,
run through the grass now and kiss me."

Abraham Lincoln 66
Acorns 195
After the Farm Auction 158
All Things to All People 393
Ambition 397
Ancestral Home 151
Angry Words 233
Animal Shelter 360
Anteaters 124
Apples 192
Apple Trees of Pioneer Grove, The 241
Apprentice Plumber 222
Art Class 244
Athlete 408
At the Charity Ball 117
At the Crossroads 371
At the Eighth-Grade Dancing Class 298
At the Home for Unwed Mothers 261
Ausagaunaskee 210

Baby 316
Bad News 50
Bad Night on Blue Hollow Road 319
Barn Burner 121
Bein' Poor 336
Bicycle Ride to the Cannery 424
Big Sister 44
Bikinis 72
Billboard 10
Bingo 157
Bird's-Eye View 92
Blackboard 162
Blues Alphabet 188
Body 204
Boogers 109
Boom Boom on B Street 199
Boozing Bigots 268
Boredom 323

Bread and Apples 85
Brother 208
Brown 299
Bubble Gum 62
Bud 301
Buffalo Nickel 255
Bull Durham 250
Bus Stop 214

Calves 152
Carnival on Eye Street 211
Carousel 102
Catfish and Watermelon 143
Chain Saw 160
Cheerleader 398
Chicago Romance, A 77
Chicken Bone 345
Chicken Milk 149
Child Abuse 236
Child in the House 260
Child Molester 374
Chinese Restaurant 276
Christmas Tree, The 381
Civil War, The 359
Class Reunion 342
Cleaning Up the Yard 337
Cloakrooms 230
Clowns 404
Cob Shed 246
Cocktail Party 280
Cold Front 290
Coming Down 392
Common Sense 395
Community Hospital 265
Company Lunchroom 383
Composition 368
Concert 40
Corn and Beans 100
Cornfield Virgin 23
Cornhusk Dolls 215
Country Smoke 29
County Road K 42
County Seat 1

Cow in the Creek 282
Coy 388
Crayola 20
Crazy in California 130
Creative Writing 407
Cricket 191
Crippled Poet's Dream, The 155
Crossing Gates 163

Damned Pretty Rain, A 197
Deluge 400
Depressed After Being Fired from Another Job 220
Devotion 58
Diary 364
Diesels 377
Diminuendo in Green 69
Dimples 306
Dog on the Stairs 164
Domestic 131
Don't Stop the Carnival 309
Doorbell 426
Downtown 217
Dream of Old, A 186
Driving to Town 238
Drought 8
Drummers 296
Duets 284

Eight O'clock in the Evening 358
Electric Avenue 13
Empty Beer Can 245
Epitaph 71
Escaping the Holy Rollers 307

Falling Apart 228
Fall of 1956 340
Famous 127
Fat 273
Father and Son 235
Fatherly Advice 399
Federal Highway 378
Fender Sitting 291
Fighter, The 414

Fire and Water 277
Fire Dream 202
Fir Tree 181
Fishing in the Rain 12
Flowers and Smoke 82
Flower Thief 212
Fool in Love, A 172
Foreclosure 78
Foreign Affairs 372
Forgiven 308
For the Record 93
Four Bottles of White Wine 185
Four Rows of Sweet Corn 248
Fourteen Stones 154
Freight Trains in Winter 175
Friendly Persuasion 343
Friend to Friend 348
From a Big Chief Tablet Found Under a Bench at the
    Courthouse Square 108
Front Porch Swing 418
Funeral Home 65

Getting at the Truth 28
Getting Caught 101
Going Steady 315
Gold 321
Golden Wedding Anniversary 156
Gone with the Grain 5
Goodbye 283
Gospel 105
Gossip 256
Grass Roots 179
Great-Grandmother's Speech on New Year's Eve 370
Greenhorn 218
Guilt 53
Guitar Strings 387

Half a Loaf 270
Happy Hour 289
Hard Cider 11
Harvest Dust 86
Hat, The 139
Having Fun with Dick and Jane 350

Hearing an Old Song Again 166
Heat Wave 318
Her Dying Child 396
High School Blues 281
Homecoming Game 322
Home from the River 106
Home from Work 420
Homework 171
Horse Opera 98
Hotel Tall Corn 113
Hot Rod 33
Housekeeper's Story, The 263
Howling Walter 184
Humor 54
Husband 338

Ice and Snow 353
Ice Cream Store 243
Ida May and Ida May Not 326
Illinois Farmers 206
Impotence 344
Incompatibility 386
In Fear of Old Age 112
Initiation 390
In Krebs's Kandy Kitchen 279
Insomnia 120
In the Barbershop 148
In the Middle of the Middle West 425
"In the Mood" 251
In Therapy 330

Jane's Blue Jeans 22
Jazz Night 64
Jericho Township 410
Jogging 61
Juney Love 35
Just the Facts 366

Kafka 332
Keeping On 60
Kids 422

Last Day of Summer Vacation, 1934   174
Last House on Union Street   134
Last Morning   292
Leaning Barn   335
Lemonade   327
Letter to Grandma   385
Lionel the Cat   17
Little Theater   14
Living in the Middle   4
Lonesome   331
Looking at Clouds   48
Loony   411
Lovers' Quarrel   295
Lyman's Way   252

Man Talking to Himself   147
Manuscript   229
Man Who Played Clarinet in the High School Band
    Back in 1936, but Then Never Amounted to
    Anything Much After That, Is Here Again Today,
    Folks, The   351
Memorial Day   285
Memo to the Erie Lackawanna   144
Me, Myself, and I   31
Mischief   317
Monopoly   415
Moonlight Yodel   125
Moony   200
Motherless Child, A   367
Motorcycle Accident   111
Mourning Dove   423
Mud, Oil, and Jello   114
Murder   320
Muscles   118

Names   34
National Pastime   391
Neighbor   126
Neighborhood   329
Newcomer   242
Nicolette   232
Nightmare   379
Night Work   16

Ninety-Two in the Shade 314
Noon at Carl's Mainline Cafe 416
North 107
North Woods 394
Nostalgia 267
Nuts and Bolts 81

Oddball 138
Old Man 183
One Tough Hombre 234
One-Way Conversation with a Rug Beater 193
Opera House 352
Opinion 328
Opposite Sex, The 99
Ordinary Sinner, An 51
Osage Orange 272
Outside the Western Auto Store 239
Out to Lunch 56

Parties 363
Peanut Butter 303
Pennies 46
Piano 182
Picking the Garbage 216
Pickle Puss 189
Pisces Sun 24
Pool Players, The 176
Postcard to Florida 38
Pregnant 198
Private Dancer 140
Puberty 88
Public Library 402
Punch Bowl 226
Putting Off the Encyclopedia Salesman 91

Questions and Answers 168

Railroad Strike 119
Rainbow 52
Rain Check 83
Red Depot, The 43
Red Dress, The 96
Redneck 354

Reds 57
Remembering the Thirties 97
Requiem 224
Retirement 305
Return to River Street 333
Revelation 389
Rocking 68
Rocking Horse 376
Roots 384
Rose Petals 135
Rose Tattoo 18

Sad 334
Sailor 254
Saturday Afternoon on Elm Street 150
Scarecrow 70
School Board 205
School Day Afternoon 167
Schoolteacher 196
Scotch Pine 190
Scratch 382
Screwdrivers 347
Second Shift at the Printing Plant 310
Seen and Not Heard 223
Senility 87
September Moon 428
Seventy-Five 300
Sheet Music 32
Shipping Clerk 324
Sick Before Supper 373
Silent 380
Simple Words 142
Sleeping Bags 165
Slow Day at the Office 302
Smell of Lilacs, The 116
Snowman 288
Some Come Running 137
Son 278
Spanish Peanuts 75
Spider Webs 128
Spittoon 266
Spooks 240
Sprinkler 419

Staring into Winter 47
Staying Up Late 264
Stocking Tops 55
Stories in the Kitchen 178
Student 339
Stuttering Hands 30
Subdivision 406
Suicide Note 356
Summer Employment 227
Summer of 1932 21
Sun Belt 412
Sunday Comics 259
Sunflower Queen 225

Tables and Chairs 249
Taking Down the Flag 213
Taking the Census 3
Tale of the Tub 312
Talk at Rukenbrod's, The 36
Talkers 274
Talking About the Erstwhile Paperboy to the
    Editor of the *Alliance Gazette* 133
Tallgrass Township 39
Telephone 294
Television 304
Thanksgiving 146
Then and Now 7
Things and Stuff 286
Thinking of Cancer 76
Thirteen 90
Tickets 80
Time Clock 41
Toilet Paper 362
Tornado Warning 405
Toy Soldiers 170
Tractor on Main Street 159
Trademarks 207
Trash 355
Trip to the Bank, A 413
Trotters 258
Tune Box 84
Two on the Farm 110

Under a Gigantic Sky 132
Unemployed 94
Union Soldier, The 122

Vacationland 311
Vision, The 271
Visiting Writer 153
V-J Day 26

War of the Hybrids 74
Wedding Reception 262
Weeping 145
Wet Spring, Dark Earth 49
Wet Towels 169
White Man's Flies 357
Why He Didn't Repair the Bookcase 346
Widower Turns Eighty, The 194
Wife Killer 136
Wild Asparagus 221
Windy 6
Winged Seeds 231
Woman in the Rented Room, The 180
Working on the Railroad 269
Worms 203
Wrestler 25
Writing Down the Dream 63

Yellow 104

ABOUT THE AUTHOR

Dave Etter lives in Elburn, Illinois, with his wife and son, four cats, and a very large collection of jazz albums. He works in a textbook publisher's warehouse in nearby St. Charles.

BOOKS BY DAVE ETTER

Go Read the River (1966)

The Last Train to Prophetstown (1968)

Strawberries (1970)

Voyages to the Inland Sea (with John Knoepfle and Lisel Mueller, 1971)

Crabtree's Woman (1972)

Well You Needn't: The Thelonious Monk Poems (1975)

Bright Mississippi (1975)

Central Standard Time: New and Selected Poems (1978)

Alliance, Illinois (1978)

Open to the Wind (1978)

Riding the Rock Island Through Kansas (1979)

Cornfields (1980)

West of Chicago (1981)

Boondocks (1982)

Alliance, Illinois (Second Edition, 1983)

Home State (1985)

Live at the Silver Dollar (1986)

Selected Poems (1987)

Midlanders (1988)

Electric Avenue (1988)

Carnival (1990)

Sunflower County (1994)